Fire For The Choir

Motivation For Choir Members

Ellis Dillard Thompson

CSS Publishing Company, Inc., Lima, Ohio

FIRE FOR THE CHOIR

Library of Congress Cataloging-in-Publication Data

Thompson, Ellis Dillard, 1924-
    Fire for the choir : motivation for choir members / Ellis Dillard Thompson.
        p. cm.
    ISBN 0-7880-1765-9 (alk. paper)
    1. Music in churches. 2. Choirs (Music) I. Title.

ML3001 .T46 2000
264'.2—dc21   00-034311
                                                                                    CIP

For more information about CSS Publishing Company resources, visit our website at www.
csspub.com, email us at csr@csspub.com, or call (800) 241-4056.

ISBN: 0-7880-1765-9   PRINTED IN USA

Dedication

I dedicate my love, peace in Christ, and this book to my dear wife Sonia, my son Jeff, and my daughter Lee Anne. I give thanks for the many years we have served in the music ministry as a family.

Sonia has been by my side for the entire thirty years of my music ministry. She served in many different capacities over the years including singer, soloist, robe caretaker, librarian, children's choir director, co-director of youth choir, singer in recording sessions, and much-revered public relations specialist in spreading love and a caring attitude to everyone.

My son Jeff experienced the music ministry from children's choirs, to youth choir, to playing clarinet in the orchestra, to writing and performing puppet shows for the children's choirs, to being finally a very strong bass in the adult choir and in recording sessions.

My daughter Lee Anne sang almost before she walked. She even experienced an extra year in the first grade choir. She started a year early while in kindergarten since her mother was the director of that choir. She had to sit somewhere during rehearsal! Lee Anne went on to serve in the children's, youth, and adult choirs as well as performing in recording sessions.

Serving the Lord through the ministry of music has been in itself a joy, but to serve side by side as a family over the many years has been a blessing beyond words.

E.D.T.

Foreword

I have known E. D. Thompson since 1975. I have worked with him in two different pastoral appointments, most recently at Blakemore United Methodist Church in Nashville, Tennessee.

What he writes in this book, *Fire For The Choir*, is not theory developed from research involving other choral programs. This book reflects what E. D. has believed and practiced successfully for many years. This book also reflects the faith of a man who learned early to trust in the gospel of Jesus Christ.

I recommend *Fire For The Choir* to the reader. I am convinced that it will transform the choir program of any church into a vibrant, enthusiastic, and committed choir — primarily because I have seen it work!

> The Rev. Michael D. O'Bannon
> Senior Pastor
> Belle Meade United Methodist Church
> Nashville, Tennessee

You make the winds your messengers,
Fire and flame your ministers.
— Psalm 104:4

Introduction

There was a knock on my choir room door. The church music students from a local college began filling into the church choir room. My good friend, Professor Meistersinger, who teaches in the church music department at the college, planned this field trip for his students.

After proper introductions and a few comments by some of the students — including how neat we keep our choir room as compared to theirs back home — Professor Meistersinger stated the reason for the visit.

"This week our unit of study deals with the motivation of choir members in a church music ministry. I have asked my good friend, Mr. Thompson, to share with you some of the things they are doing here at this church."

Bang! Now, I was standing on the big spot marked X. Frankly, I could have been given a much harder task. Motivation is something that I have studied and to which I have given a great deal of thought. Of course, motivation is very important. One can have a church situation with excellent facilities, superior equipment, and varied materials; but if people are not motivated to enroll, participate, and minister through the music program, then all of these other attributes are worthless.

I had done my homework. I had given some preparation as to how I would present this matter, and even how I may motivate *these* visiting students in being interested in learning what I wanted to present to them.

I simply held in my hand a list of 22 topics that I would take up with the students. I knew that I could expound on each topic extemporaneously, because each and every one of the items had worked for me in my programs. I knew that it would be easy for me to hold this list in my hand as we walked about the church facilities, having the students handle the equipment and hold materials, as we really went into depth with this matter of motivation of choir members in a church music program.

Here are the 22 topics that I presented to this class of students on that day:

1. Spirituality
2. Recruiting Members For The Music Program
3. Choir Attendance
4. Music For The Worship Service
5. Organizing A Music Library
6. Selecting Choir Officers
7. Writing A Choir Newsletter
8. M.A.R.S. (Monthly After-Rehearsal Social)
9. Annual Choir Christmas Dinner
10. A Little Bit Of Broadway
11. Making A Professional Recording

What Else?
12. We Care
13. Personal Contact
14. Membership Involvement
15. Discipline
16. Choir Children
17. Cantatas
18. Special Arrangements And Compositions
19. Composition Contest
20. Using Instrumental Music
21. Stereo Equipment
22. Musicianship

1. Spirituality

Have you ever seen a part-time choir director who ran over to the church — usually late — for the Wednesday night rehearsal, grabbed an anthem from a drawer, and said, "Well, let's do this one Sunday."?

The director then rehearsed through that anthem with his or her musical knowledge — not very interestingly, not very inspiringly. The choir members were bored with having to work so hard on just one piece of music. Even when the choir members sang it the following Sunday, they really did not feel prepared enough to enjoy serving with that piece of music, even though it may have been an excellent piece of music.

The organist should not have the attitude of being a recitalist either. Nor should the choir just give a concert on Sunday.

Now, think of the choir where serving and worshiping God is the focal point. Sit in this choir where the love, caring attitudes, and the Spirit of God reside. Rehearse that same piece of music mentioned above, and see how the text and the music *now* exert a glow and a force of inspiration to all present.

This type of leadership is the job of the choir director. All of us are still growing in the knowledge and the wisdom of our God. Some are further along than others.

In First Corinthians, the Apostle Paul says: "I fed you with milk, not solid food, for you were not ready for solid food. Even now you are still not ready, for you are still of the flesh ..." (1 Corinthians 3:2-3).

When I have talked to some groups, I have gone to the chalk board and drawn a line perpendicular to the floor. I have said that this line represents our growth in the knowledge and wisdom of God — our spiritual growth. At the bottom point of the line we have the sinner who has separated himself or herself from God. The tip top point of the line represents the saint of the highest order. Almost all of us are somewhere in between. Wherever we are, we are trying to advance *up* that line through prayer, by reading and studying the Holy Scripture, and with constant self-reflection, evaluation, attitude adjustment, and meditation.

The music program, including all of the choirs, is part of the church. It is part of the Body of Christ. The minister of music is the designated leader over this holy institution. Full-time or part-time, a choir director can serve in a way that brings spirituality to the music ministry serving the choirs and other musical organizations, the congregation, and the community.

A quote from Cliff Barrows in the March 1982 issue of *Decision* magazine says it very well: "As far as the attitude of the choir is concerned, the musician in charge is the key...."

Cliff went on in his article to say that the directors set the pattern by their own personal lives, and their relationships with the Lord in their earnest and honest commitment. The choir will follow his or her leadership.

> *Let the word of Christ dwell in you richly; teach and admonish one another in all wisdom; and with gratitude in your hearts sing psalms, hymns, and spiritual songs to God. And whatever you do, in word or deed, do everything in the name of the Lord Jesus, giving thanks to God the Father through him.* — Colossians 3:16-17

2. Recruiting Members For The Music Program

Every choir needs to recruit new members. You can do a lot of things with regard to inviting new members into the choir. You simply call prospects or write them a note, but these things very well may not work.

Possibly you need to do many things with regard to recruiting. Caring about each person as a human being is important. Make all prospects realize that they are important and they are needed. Asking a prospect to ride to choir practice in your car can do wonders!

Here are a few things that might encourage new members to come into the choir:

1. Following the worship services, always greet new people who join the church. Let them know that you really care that they have united with your church. Present each one of them with a complimentary copy of your latest choir recording if you have done recordings. Some people whom you greet will reveal a talent and joy in singing. Some will make it known immediately that they cannot "carry a tune in a bucket." This is, at least, an initial approach.

2. You probably have had a number of visitors to your church whom you have approached about singing in the choir and they have joined. Also, you want to be on the lookout for instrumental players.

Over the years you have seen some of these visitors join the church. You probably have seen people who have gone down to the chancel at the close of a service in their choir robes and join the church. Their initial introduction to the church was by way of serving in the choir.

3. Good prospects may be contacted by a note enclosed in the latest issue of *Choir Notes* or the church newsletter. This will give the prospects information about the choirs and general music program.

4. A note should be followed always by a telephone call or a personal visit. Keep a file of your prospects.

5. Your list of good prospects may include (1) former choir members, (2) past children and youth choir members, now older, (3) prospects you hear about through other choir members, pastors, other staff members, and congregational members, and (4) names revealed through a church-wide survey.

6. You may find that the night of your M.A.R.S. (Monthly After-Rehearsal Social) is a good time to invite new prospects. On this occasion, they can meet others after rehearsal in a relaxed social environment. These new choir prospects should have seen and participated in a very efficient rehearsal and seen an attitude of spiritual caring on this first night with the choir.

7. Sometimes it is effective to have a period of time during the month of September to concentrate on enrollment in the various musical organizations. September is the beginning of a new school year. Summer vacations are over. And the Christmas season, which is an inspiring time and a musically fun time to join in the music, is approaching. Of course, year round recruiting is important.

8. As mentioned earlier, having someone go by the homes of choir prospects and bring them to their first choir practice is very effective!

9. It is appropriate to place a small notice in the church's weekly newsletter and church bulletin inviting new members into the choir. Following are six examples that may be suitable for your situation. Please feel free to use any of these notices as written, or modified, to fit your particular need:

♪ ♪ ♪ ♪ ♪

Sanctuary Choir Needs Singers
In the twelfth chapter of First Corinthians, the Apostle Paul tells us that each one of us is given spiritual gifts, or abilities, from God. There are many different kinds of spiritual gifts, but the same Spirit gives them.

Perhaps the Lord is calling YOU — NOW — to use your talents in the service of your church. Singing in the choir could be one special way to be a witness for the Lord.

The only prerequisites are that (1) you enjoy singing, (2) you are able to "carry a tune," (3) you want to learn more about music, and (4) you want to serve the church in this special way.

We would love to see you on Wednesday evening in the choir room for rehearsal at 7:30 p.m. We quit promptly at 9:00 p.m. A baby sitter will be provided if you let us know in advance.

(Your Name)
Choir Director

♪ ♪ ♪ ♪ ♪

Singers Needed In Sanctuary Choir

You don't have to read music. You don't have to have a solo-type voice. You will learn how to sing your part at the rehearsals on Wednesday nights.

We are beginning to rehearse the Christmas music, and we need YOU. We need about ten additional singers to bring our enrollment up to where it was before some of our members moved away or had to drop out for various reasons.

If you can "carry a tune" and want to serve God and your church by singing, then please come on Wednesday evening to the choir room at 7:30 p.m. We quit promptly at 9:00 p.m.

We promise that you will have fun while you learn music — fun in a Christian fellowship ...

(Your Name)
Choir Director

♪ ♪ ♪ ♪ ♪

Do You Enjoy Singing?
Can You Carry A Tune?

... then YOU are needed in the Sanctuary Choir. You don't have to know how to read music. You get that on Wednesday nights in the choir room from 7:30 p.m. until 9:00 p.m.

The Easter music is beginning to come in, and I feel that it is going to be GREAT! The music should be nice for the congregation to hear and exciting for the choir to sing. This is the time of year when you can join the choir and be right at the beginning of learning the new music.

We promise you good FUN, FELLOWSHIP, sometimes FOOD, and always the pleasure and blessing of serving your church in a very direct way.

Hope to see you on Wednesday.

(Your Name)
Choir Director

♪ ♪ ♪ ♪ ♪

If You Can "Carry A Tune"
We Need YOU In The Sanctuary Choir!

Our choir program could be an opportunity for YOU

TO GROW

TO MINISTER

TO SHARE

TO SERVE GOD

with your talent.

Attention: High School and College students:

We hope you will come and help us this summer too, as we will be having some of our regular choir members in and out on vacations.

14

If you can serve your church in this way, PLEASE COME.

(Your Name)
Choir Director

♪ ♪ ♪ ♪ ♪

Our Goal Is To Have A 40-Voice Sanctuary Choir By The End Of September.

We have set Wednesday night, September 8, as the BIG "kick-off" rehearsal. Rehearsals start promptly at 7:30 p.m. and finish precisely at 9:00 p.m. However, on September 8 please plan to stay until 9:30 to enjoy some after-rehearsal refreshments.

Come if you enjoy singing. We promise you will learn more about music and will have some real fellowship enjoyment PLUS the joy and blessings of using your talents and life to serve God and others.

On rehearsal nights, Mr. Gusto's daughter, Connie, and our son, Jeff, will be on hand to supervise and play games with your children. The "choir kids" have the time of their lives on Wednesday nights.

There are many reasons why YOU need to be among our number.

(Your Name)
Choir Director

♪ ♪ ♪ ♪ ♪

We Broke The Record!

Last Sunday the Sanctuary Choir attendance at the morning worship service broke the past record and shot the line on our wall chart up to 33. I am proud of the loyal service of this choir. The previous record was 32 in attendance. WE BROKE THE RECORD ... BY ONE!!

After the service, I told the choir that if any ONE of them had not been there, we could not have broken the record.

Don't you see how important everyONE is in the service of our church? Still, there are many good singers in the congregation who could come, join, and serve in the choir. We would love to see YOU on Wednesday night at 7:30 p.m. in the choir room.

(Your Name)
Choir Director

♪ ♪ ♪ ♪ ♪

In recruiting, you as choir director need to talk to the prospects personally. *Be enthusiastic* about the music ministry when you talk to prospects. They need to want the product that you are selling. They need to know that this service will be beneficial to them. They must realize that they will be in an *excellent* music program.

Possibly more than one contact will be required in trying to get a person interested in the music program. However, one should use good judgment in just how long or how far one goes in trying to get a person to join the choir. Nothing is more distasteful than to feel like you are being nagged. All is not lost as they may decide to join at a later date.

Do not lag in zeal, be ardent in spirit, serve the Lord. — Romans 12:11

3. Choir Attendance

Most choirs have some philosophy with regard to choir attendance. There are some choir directors who have the rule that no members can sing the worship service on Sunday unless they were present at the preceding rehearsal. I am not sure what this would do to a small choir in the middle of a flu epidemic!

Here is a system that has seemed to work over the years through sickness, summer vacation time — yes, flu epidemics!

The system is to rehearse four weeks of music in advance. Certainly no choir should perform music which is not well rehearsed anyway.

Tell your people to come on and sing whenever they can. If they are to be out of town and have to miss a week or two of rehearsals, the anthem still will be rehearsed by them if the music has been in their rehearsals folders for the four weeks. The music selections will be familiar to everyone when it comes time to present them in a worship service. Also, the final polish you give the music on the Sunday morning before the service will clear up any important pitfalls for them too.

You as the director should say, "Come on and sing! Come Wednesday night if you can't be there Sunday, and come Sunday if you weren't there on Wednesday." You should find that this system helps morale and helps attendance.

Place a calendar on your choir room bulletin board. It should be a calendar that gives space for each day in the week. Remind your choir members through your monthly issue of *Choir Notes* to pencil their name in at any date in advance that they know they will be absent from choir.

Of course, there will be times when some members will miss writing their names on the calendar because they won't know they will be absent until it is too late. They should be made aware that you understand this too. They should not feel guilty that they had to miss and didn't get their name on the calendar. Encourage them to call if possible if they see that they cannot come to a rehearsal or service and didn't have time to get it on the calendar.

You will be amazed how this system helps your program. This calendar can help plan your music if you know of particular dates when certain members will be missing. Also, the choir members will sense another part of your good organizational devices which indeed helps their morale, sense of belonging, and being a part of a successful music program.

You can't make a person come to choir, but you can motivate so that the person wants to come regularly.

When people need to miss a rehearsal because of work, or go see the new grandbaby, or see a nephew graduate from college, then use this information as an opportunity to tell them how happy you are for them. Let them know that we really care and that they are important ... and the choir director has a good news item to go in the next issue of *Choir Notes*!

> *I will sing to the Lord as long as I live; I will sing praise to my God while I have being.*
> — Psalm 104:33

4. Music For The Worship Service

"Are we singing only one thing today?" This was said in a disappointed way by one of the singers as she entered the choir room on Sunday morning.

We should motivate the choir members by utilizing their talents. Sad is the choir which strolls in to the service, seemingly in utter confusion as they look for their chairs, and then they sing only one piece of music during the service. The choir members have come to serve, so let them come and sing!

Choir members will be motivated to serve and "keep on keeping on" if they feel that they are important to the worship services and are making a real contribution.

Choir members might sing five things during a service. This is in addition to their important role in leading good hymn singing. *They have come to serve, so let them come and sing!* Of course, this might be altered from time to time by the format and type of worship service.

Choral Call To Worship

A Choral Call To Worship or Introit begins the worship service. The type of service may dictate the type of Introit. Sometimes it could be effective to have a big, broad musical expression marked *forte*. At other times a very reverent, smooth, quiet statement may do the best job to open the worship.

These Choral Calls To Worship can be found published by some music publishers. Also, a resourceful director can go into the anthem file and pull out excerpts that will do a superior job. Also, many good Introits can be found in your church hymnal.

These pieces of music should strengthen the opening of the service and contribute to the unique worship of the congregation. Yes, this also motivates the choir members. The choir members will realize that they are serving a definite purpose in achieving this goal of giving of their best to their Maker in beginning a worship of praise to our God.

The choir will want to do even a short Introit with real quality and meaning.

Choral Call To Prayer

A piece of music with a meaningful text which is sung before the prayer is a Choral Call To Prayer. Sometimes it is effective to sing a Prayer Response with an Amen following a prayer.

Again, excerpts from anthems may be used. An excerpt from many hymns from the hymnal can be effective before or after prayer.

Try not to do the same response too often. Having a different one each Sunday adds to the worship. Also, choir members have something different to sing each week. As a director, be alert as to whether the piece of music chosen should be accompanied or sung *a cappella*.

This prayer music should enhance the worship and make the verbal prayer most effective.

Anthems

"Are we singing only one thing today?" She almost sounded like there was no point in her coming. The choir traditionally might sing two anthems during a worship service. This will motivate your choir members. Of course, the type of worship service or the size and ability of the choir will determine whether you use one or two anthems. If only one anthem is to be done, see to it that the anthem chosen is one which has the spiritual and musical power to motivate members to come and sing their hearts out as well as thrill and inspire the congregation.

You may be requested by the church or your pastor to do two anthems at some worship services. You will find success in choosing appropriate anthems which contrast. For instance, if one anthem is big and powerful, the other should be quiet and *legato*. You may contrast a fast tempo with a slow one. You can contrast a classic with a contemporary piece of music. Of course, the appropriateness and the message are always of utmost importance.

You may find that your choir will be excited and inspired to do a variety of music. Many styles of music also call for varied rehearsal techniques as well as interpretations. You should not perform a Mozart piece of the eighteenth century the same as a Brahms piece of the nineteenth century. There are many styles within the twentieth century. There is a choice of good and bad taste in performing much of the inspirational or gospel music.

Never be afraid to musically uplift your choir and your congregation. However, extreme dissonance in your music may turn off even some of your more schooled singers and congregational members. Perhaps you should not perform some ancient motet just because you studied it in a musicology class. But there is a wealth of great inspirational music from the masters' pens of Bach, Handel, Haydn, Mozart, Beethoven, Mendelssohn, Schubert, Brahms, and on and on, as well as good twentieth century composers.

I judged a high school choral festival a while back. Many of the directors had tried "cute" things to perform in contest to try to get a high rating — some of it was good music and some bad. Toward the close of the day, a director came on stage with his choir and performed the "Hallelujah Chorus" from *Mount of Olives* by Beethoven. The choir completed the performance, almost bringing the house down with applause. The listeners liked what they heard from little seventh graders to grandparents in the audience. The director passed by my table and I said, "Nice job." He smiled and replied, "You can't beat art." I think he's right.

All of us need to be in constant touch with new publications by being members of publishers' choral library mailings, and by listening to lots and lots of recordings. Always be aware that we need to be our own resource person in knowing music literature of all types.

There is a lot of worshipful music being published today. Do yourself a favor and read the section on what makes a piece of music "good music" in a book called *Music and Worship in the Church* by Lovelace and Rice, published by Abingdon Press. Lovelace and Rice make a very potent statement when they write: "Some people consider music only as entertainment, but they thereby relegate art to a place of relative unimportance. Great music is not an embellishment of life but a spiritual enrichment of it. It is a vital factor of expression, just as religion is a central, not a peripheral, matter."

Benedictional Response

Some worship services close by only a spoken benediction. Some close with a hymn. Some services close with the people kneeling at the chancel or before the altar. You know your own church and congregation and what is needed. If you feel that a piece of music at the end of the service following the spoken benediction is a way of enhancing the worship, then you may want to use a choral Benedictional Response.

You can buy good responses, you can find excerpts in anthems and hymns, you can write them, and you may have the congregation sing them with the choir.

A short time ago I visited a church service where I experienced a beautiful closing to the worship as people came and stood or knelt before the altar and sang with the choir. It was very moving and spiritually meaningful.

In addition to the choir singing alone, many hymnals and other resources offer a wealth of material for the choir and congregation to sing responses *antiphonally*, and to use a cantor with congregational responses.

The church pastor and the minister of music should work closely together at all times. This can make all music including responses have a very special meaning and fit into the worship service to the best possible advantage in serving the worshipful experience of the congregation.

The choir's purpose is not just to sing; the music must show the way to our Savior. We cannot display music for art's sake while human lives around us have not yet found the harmony of God's love, peace, and salvation.

Dream a little when you plan your worship music. Envision how the music will affect the congregation and your choir members as they sing it. As you think and dream, the Holy Spirit will dream with you. You will be amazed at the ideas and inspirations

22

that will come into your mind while you plan the music for the worship service.

Always be flexible. During the service if you feel that the worship is being led in a different direction, don't hesitate to delete, insert, or change from your printed bulletin.

And, remember, successful experiences *motivate* your choir members.

> *It was the duty of the trumpeters and singers to make themselves heard in unison in praise and thanksgiving to the Lord ... for the glory of the Lord filled the house of God.*
> — 2 Chronicles 13-14

To Thee I Pray

Before or After Prayer

From Psalm 5

Ellis D. Thompson

O give ear to my words, O God;

Oo

Hear-ken to the sound of my cry, My God.

Ah

Ah

My God.

To Thee I pray, Lead my life. { To Thee, O God, I pray. / A - men. }

(The publisher grants permission for you to make multiple copies of this choral Call To Prayer OR Prayer Response for use with your church choir.)

5. Organizing A Music Library

Another way your music program can reveal professionalism is by organizing and maintaining a well-structured music library. This will motivate your choir members by allowing them to be a part of a well-organized music program.

When a new choral anthem enters the music library of the church choir, there are a number of things which need to be done to handle the new music efficiently.

First of all, you will want each choir member to be given the exact same piece of music each and every time the selection is used in a rehearsal and worship service. Each piece of music should be given a number which will correspond to the number of a specific choir member's music folder.

This will allow the choir members to receive the exact piece of music on which they have placed their own penciled-in instructions which they have learned from past choir rehearsals.

The best system of assigning numbers to the choir members is first assign the choir member with a choir robe that fits well. The number of that robe will also be the number of the choir member's rehearsal folder, and the choir member's performance folder.

Then, the number of each anthem placed into the music folders will bear that same number assigned to that specific choir member.

The following guidelines may be helpful to follow each time a new anthem is purchased for the choir:

1. Stamp the back cover or other appropriate place on each anthem with a rubber stamp stating the name of the church choir, and the church address under the large letters MUSIC LIBRARY.

2. Number each anthem plainly and large enough to be seen on the front of each anthem.

3. Fill out three cards to be placed in your card catalog with regard to this anthem. One card should be filed by the **title** of the

anthem. A second card should be filed by the name of the **composer** and/or **arranger**. A third card should be filed by the **character** of the music, such as: General use, Advent, Baptism, Christmas, Easter, Holy Communion, Lent, Palm Sunday, Pentecost, and others.

4. When the musical selection is ready to be used, place each anthem in the rehearsal folders of the choir members. The number on the anthem, of course, corresponds with the number assigned to each choir member's music folder.

5. During rehearsals, each choir member is free to write in with pencil any needed expression or interpretation marks. Stress that only pencil marks be used. No ink pens! Each rehearsal folder should be equipped with a good soft pencil with a good eraser. Often, a person's marks may need to be erased or changed.

6. After the anthem has been presented during a worship service, the anthem should be turned in by each choir member. An efficient way to handle this is to have a box or wire basket in the choir room for the choir members to place their piece of music after it has been used.

7. When the anthem comes out of the music folders, the music librarian should arrange the numbered music from 1 through 40, or whatever number of copies you have. Place them in a large library envelope or folder, and write on the front of the envelope the date the anthem was used.

8. File the music envelope in your music cabinet to be ready for the next time the anthem is needed.

These guidelines should keep your music library in an excellent functioning condition.

The above guidelines refer directly to choral anthems. Of course, all music should be handled in a similar manner.

Your music library should organize the music for children's choirs, youth choir, handbell choirs, instrumental ensembles, orchestral arrangements, cantatas, oratorios, anthem or choral response collections, and recordings.

But all things should be done decently and in order.
— 1 Corinthians 14:40

6. Selecting Choir Officers

Most organizations elect officers. Sometimes it is done as a formality rather than as a real functional need. Real success comes from an election of people to serve in a definite capacity — to have a definite job to do.

The particular needs in your church may warrant more, fewer, or even different officers; however, the following slate of officers should be able to function effectively in fulfilling the necessary duties required in the operation of a well-organized choir program.

The **president** of the choir should hold an office in which honor is felt. It is a position that exercises definite leadership. All during the year there will be times when this leadership will have an input in decisions, in working out problems, and even in being creative in initiating exciting ventures in an ongoing, enterprising organization that a church choir should be.

There are times when the choir director will be occupied with musical matters and matters of worship. The director should be very happy to leave certain matters with the president of the choir, such as making needed contacts, holding a meeting, writing a letter, making a telephone call, or arriving at a solution. Also, the choir president should serve on the church's music committee and worship committee, if the church has these.

The choir president takes the initiative in such matters as making presentations at your monthly socials and Christmas dinners. Over the weeks and months, there are many things that will come up if the choir is truly an "up and at 'em," meaningful, and doing organization.

As a personal experience, once our choir president came to me explaining that an orchestra member's 'cello had been accidentally damaged following a rehearsal with the choir. Feeling some responsibility, our president suggested a way in which we could help this musician with the expense of repairing her 'cello. It was this president's feeling of leadership that prompted him to be concerned and to come up with a workable solution. A good choir president can be an asset to any organization.

A **vice-president** should be elected in your choir. As in the tradition, this person serves in the absence of the president. However, because this really gives this officer very little to do, it is wise to give this person some other needed responsibility. The choir director can easily think of a job that would take some work off of him or her in the functioning of the choir program.

It depends who the person is, but it may be a person who could take charge of the bulletin boards. The choir room bulletin boards need to have new items posted, out of date items removed, and pictures displayed properly. This can be a real enjoyment to the choir members.

The choir **secretary** should be a person who can keep a very neat and accurate roll book. The roll book should contain a page for each choir member on which is noted his or her name, address, telephone numbers at home and work, choir part sung, and birthday month. On this sheet the secretary keeps an accurate record of attendance at all rehearsals and worship services.

Why is this roll book so important? As choir director you have two very important reasons for using it. First of all, you have a visual record of a person's attendance. If choir members have been absent, you can see exactly how many times they have missed. You will want to contact those members personally if they have been missing choir. This contacting should not be done by the secretary. The choir director needs to contact the members personally.

At the end of each month, the secretary will hand to the director a list of all the members who had perfect attendance for the month and those who missed only one time during the month at either a rehearsal or a service. Special recognition may be given to these people in the monthly issue of *Choir Notes*. Also, the attendance percentage is figured following a month of record keeping to be published in the *Choir Notes*. (See section 5 in the chapter on "Writing A Choir Newsletter.")

In your church choir the secretary may be the person who orders flowers to be sent to a member who has had a death in the immediate family, or sends a gift on an appropriate occasion. The secretary may write a card to be sent to someone who is sick. The secretary might pass the card around for each choir member to sign and write in a personal "one-liner." Yes, the choir secretary has an important job to fulfill.

Consider electing an **assistant secretary** to take the roll and do all of the above when the choir secretary is absent, sick, or on vacation. This gets another person involved.

The choir **treasurer** handles the money in the choir treasury. This is not referring to the music budget of the church. But the choir should have a little money on reserve in its treasury. You would not necessarily have enough to open a checking account at the bank.

Assessing the choir members a fee is probably not wise. However, the choir treasurer may place a hat on the table at your monthly after rehearsal socials, and anyone who is so inclined may make a small donation. You do need a small amount of money in the choir treasury to purchase get well cards, flowers, gifts, refreshments, and, on occasion, give to the memorial fund of the church in honor or in memory of someone.

The **social chairperson** needs to be a good organizer. This person will coordinate the after rehearsal social each month, the annual Christmas dinner, and any other social event.

It may be traditional for your full sanctuary choir to sing for two morning worship services on Easter Sunday. You may find it to be a lot of fun to have orange juice and something to eat following the first service and before Sunday School classes begin. Of course, the social chairperson would play a great role in the event your choir held a summer retreat or snack supper in conjunction with an extra rehearsal before the Christmas cantata performance or a similar happening.

In your church choir program you may want to have three additional officers which are appointed rather than elected. These are librarian, robe caretaker, and chaplain. In your particular situation, it may be that you would want to elect these three officers.

The choir **librarian** needs to be a person with the abilities and the desire to handle the job. The librarian should work closely with the choir director with regard to what music needs to go into the rehearsal folders, and what music should be taken out. Music which comes out needs to be dated as to when it was used, and then properly filed away.

The card catalog needs to be kept up to date. Each anthem and choral response should be cross-indexed three ways. You will often need to refer to the cards with titles, cards with composer's or arranger's name, and cards revealing the character of the music — Advent, Baptism, Christmas, Easter, Holy Communion, Lent, Palm Sunday, Pentecost, and so on.

The librarian may call on help from other choir members in doing these many jobs. This gets more people involved and interested in the choir program.

New music that comes in needs to be stamped with a rubber stamp identifying the music library and church name. The anthems need to be numbered so that each choir member receives his or her same numbered piece of music to go in the numbered rehearsal folders each time the anthem is used. The *penciled* instruction marks which the singers write on their parts during rehearsal will be there each time they rehearse that selection. Always adhere to the musician's rule: *never write on music with ink!*

The choir **robe caretaker** needs to be a person who will take an interest in assigning the choir robes and who will handle all matters pertaining to the choir robes.

When a new person joins the choir, that person needs to be assigned a robe that fits. Often a visitor will come to sing with the choir. That person needs to be efficiently fitted in a choir robe with proper stole and all other accessories. Instrumentalists who perform with the choir in worship services will need to be fitted in robes.

When a church purchases new choir robes, the manufacturer places a number on the inside of each robe next to the tag which states the size. This number is the robe number.

The best system of assigning robes to the members is to assign the same robe number as the choir member's rehearsal music folder. This can be accomplished easily by assigning the robe which fits the person first, and then assigning the rehearsal music folder with that same number.

The robe caretaker is the person responsible for carrying out the desire of the church to have the robes and stoles cleaned and mended when needed.

The choir robe caretaker is the person everyone looks to in serving all needed matters regarding the choir robes and accessories.

Consider having a choir **chaplain.** You should find a need for this person within the church choir. The choir director often will find responsibilities that can be given to the chaplain. The choir should be a caring group of people, and this is an extension of seeing that all choir members enjoy this caring attitude.

At the conclusion or beginning of rehearsals, the chaplain may share the responsibility with the director and other members in bringing a beautiful prayer to begin the rehearsal or to end your day. Remember in the prayer the sick, grieved, and troubled ones that are brought to the choir's attention. In fact, every person in the choir has cares that need to be ministered to.

Yes, the choir chaplain fulfills a need. To cite a personal experience — one night we were busily rehearsing in the choir room when all of a sudden the door flew open and a young man ran in. He abruptly reached over and grabbed a piece of music from one of the singers, sat down, and began singing off-key at the top of his lungs. Later we found out that he was a mental patient from a local facility and had found his way into the church.

What actually happened was that I, as choir director, continued in my place before the choir in rehearsal, and our choir chaplain took this young man outside, talked with him, and gave him all of the love and attention he could. A phone call to the young man's parents ended the episode in a very quiet, compassionate, Christian love solution. I was grateful for our choir chaplain on that night.

This group of choir officers named above, along with the choir director and organist, may form what can be called the choir **executive committee.** The committee may meet when the need arises and make the necessary decisions that can be taken to the other members.

Prayerfully select the choir officers. Pray for them after they have been selected.

> ... tend the flock of God that is in your charge, exercising the oversight, not under compulsion but willingly, as God would have you do it — not for sordid gain but eagerly. Do not lord it over those in your charge, but be examples to the flock.
> — 1 Peter 5:2-3

7. Writing A Choir Newsletter

Have you ever sung in a choir in which the director stood there and talked and talked on and on when the choir really wanted to sing?

There are some things that do need to be said. There are some announcements that must be made. Yes, there even have to be some things spoken that help the motivation of the choir members in the rehearsal. But talking on and on will not get it!

As the director, why not have a newsletter sent to each member of the choir every month and do your talking there? Make your announcements. In fact, publicize coming events with such enthusiasm that they are anticipated with real excitement.

You may want to call your newsletter something other than *Choir Notes*. What is it? It simply is a written communication to your choir members. You may want to call it your *Choir Newsletter,* or *Monthly Choir Announcements*, or *Music Notes*. Whatever you call it, the purpose is to *communicate*.

A monthly issue does the job of lining up the work for a month. There are times when you absolutely have to get out an important announcement to everyone in between the monthly issues. So, you can get out a short *Choir Half Note*. You may add "1/2" to the previous issue number.

Sometimes you could write "Extra" at the beginning.

The following is an example:

♪ ♪ ♪ ♪ ♪

♪ CHOIR NOTES ♪
(Name of Church)
(City and State)
Volume ?, Number ? 1/2 (Date)

I will sing to the Lord as long as I live; I will sing praise to my God while I have being.
— Psalm 104:33

EXTRA   EXTRA   EXTRA

February offers a special opportunity to serve
Wednesday, February 16
Ash Wednesday Service

Combined Choirs To Sing

On Wednesday evening the West Nashville Parish churches will combine for a worship service at 7:00 p.m. in our sanctuary. Choirs from the participating churches have been invited to join in singing John Stainer's "God So Loved the World."

So — 6:30 p.m. rehearsal is very important that evening. The schedule for February 16 will be:

6:00 p.m. — Supper (Fellowship Hall)

6:30 p.m. — Combined Choir rehearsal (Choir room)

7:00 p.m. — Worship Service (Sanctuary)

It should be a very nice evening. This will be our first service in Lent.

After the service, could we remove our robes and stay in the choir room about 15 minutes just to run through the music we will be doing for Sunday? Thanks.

See you this WEDNESDAY.

♪ ♪ ♪ ♪ ♪

Some choir directors waste a lot of valuable rehearsal time by standing before the choir and talking. Choir members will resent having to waste their time even though the director is making statements and announcements that need to be said. Use your rehearsal time to rehearse music, and use your *Choir Notes* to make your announcements.

If you ever do have to stop during a rehearsal and have an important business meeting, you will be amazed as to how attentive the members will be in as much as this type of interruption happens so infrequently.

What do you write in the *Choir Notes*? Here are a few things that should make good readable *Choir Notes*.

1. Begin with a personal "note." You may give it the unique heading: **A "Note" From The Choir Director**.

A colleague of mine uses the heading: **My Thoughts.** You may want to use some other well-suited heading. At any rate, some of your thoughts can be very interesting to the choir members and can inspire, teach and *motivate* the members.

Here is an example:

♪ ♪ ♪ ♪ ♪

♪ A "Note" From The Choir Director ♪
I taught school in South Carolina a number of years ago, and I learned something from an old country judge that I have never forgotten.

This kind, likeable old judge was asked to teach a Sunday school class. On Sunday morning, two gentlemen showed him to his room. The old judge stood in the doorway, looked around, and then said, "It's not big enough."

So, the men without hesitation took the judge to a larger room and told him that he could teach his class in this room. The old judge stood at the door looking around the room with his very stern but expressive eyes. He then looked up at the two men accompanying him, and said, "It's not big enough."

At this point, the two gentlemen with the judge looked at each other rather quizzically; but, without saying a word, they moved on down to the end of the building to the Fellowship Hall. Each gentleman swung open one of the double doors to the large Fellowship Hall. The smiles quickly disappeared from their faces as the old judge said, "It's not big enough."

Now, these two gentlemen with the judge said nothing, but their expressions obviously revealed the thought that the judge had lost his mind. It was interesting to see that the judge still possessed his pleasant smile. He lacked any signs of frustration and had a confident walk as the three headed down the hall.

One of the gentleman said, "The church has recently purchased an old warehouse next door which we want to build into a gym and a large assembly hall and dining hall. We will show that to you."

At this point I am sure that each of the men (except the judge) thought that this was silly and out of the question.

As the three men strolled into the spaciousness of the old warehouse to become a gymnasium, the old judge's smile became broader and broader as he walked over the entire floor. He stopped, looked at the two gentlemen, and said, "This is where I shall teach my class."

Not only these two gentlemen, but others certainly must have thought how ridiculous this idea was. How could he hope to fill this spaciousness with his class?

Well, to make a long story much shorter, the truth is that within a few months of the dynamic teaching of this old, wise judge and Bible teacher, they had to start moving in extra chairs and the radio station in town asked permission to broadcast his Sunday school lesson each Sunday morning.

I saw this find old judge downtown on the square one day. I asked him about this. His answer was simple. He said, "Son, if you don't expect much, then you aren't gonna get much."

Well, I expect forty voices enrolled in the sanctuary choir by the end of September. Come on down. We've got the room!

E. D. Thompson
Choir Director

♪ ♪ ♪ ♪ ♪

(**Editor's note:** The above is an example of what you may choose to use in your column, "A 'Note' From The Choir Director."

In the Appendix you will find twenty additional "Notes" which this writer has written to his choirs over the years. You may use any of these as a pattern in your work, or possibly read as inspirational pieces.)

2. In each issue of the *Choir Notes*, announce the important **Upcoming Events** to take place during the months ahead. For instance, a special service could be emphasized, or a reminder that the choir will sing both services on Easter Sunday morning, or a final rehearsal with handbells for Christmas will take place at a certain time and place.

Sometimes the event will be such that you might state it in the form of a headline above "A 'Note' From The Choir Director." The important thing is to announce all events which you need the choir members to know about. The events should be listed in a chronological order. Maybe add a reminder to cut out the schedule and place it on the kitchen bulletin board at home.

Here is an example:

♪ ♪ ♪ ♪ ♪

Upcoming Events

**Combined choirs will sing for both services
on Easter Sunday**

Other opportunities to serve during Lent

The combined Sanctuary and Youth choirs will
be singing both services on Easter Sunday, April 3.
Clip out this schedule and post it on your
kitchen bulletin board as a reminder.

Wednesday, March 16
Regular choir rehearsal
7:30 - 9:00 p.m.

Sunday, March 20
Combined choir rehearsal in the sanctuary
3:00 - 5:00 p.m.

Wednesday, March 23
Regular choir rehearsal
7:30 - 9:00 p.m.

Sunday, March 27
Palm Sunday worship service
11:00 a.m.

Sunday, March 27
Soloists rehearse with organ and string quartet
3:00 p.m.

Wednesday, March 30
Combined choir rehearsal with brass ensemble
7:30 - 9:00 p.m. in the sanctuary

Thursday, March 31
Maundy Thursday Communion service
7:30 p.m.

Friday, April 1
Good Friday worship service
7:30 p.m.

Sunday, April 3
Easter Sunday worship services
8:00 a.m. and 11:00 a.m.

Mark Your Calendars ...

Drop by the choir room following the 8:00 a.m. service on Easter for some orange juice, a surprise from Betty's nutritional kitchen, and a little fellowship before Sunday School.

** The most glorious season
in the lives of Christians **

Mark your calendars *now* to come and serve the Lord with gladness ... CHRIST IS ALIVE!

♪ ♪ ♪ ♪ ♪

3. Include in each month's issue of *Choir Notes* the announcement of the coming month's **M.A.R.S.** with date, time, and place. (See the next chapter in this book about the **M**onthly **A**fter-**Re**hearsal **S**ocial.)

The following is an example you might include in your monthly issue of *Choir Notes*:

♪ ♪ ♪ ♪ ♪

M.A.R.S.
(Monthly After-Rehearsal Social)

M.A.R.S. for JUNE: Wednesday, June 23

Happy June Birthday to: Andy Andante, Chris Crescendo, Lisa Legato, Mark Marcato, and Mary Mezzo.

For our June M.A.R.S. we have been invited to the home of Margaret and Mark Marcato. They live at 1750 Bach Blvd. Closer to the time we shall supply you with a map and exact instructions as to how to get there — OR, as, always, if you would feel more comfortable by going with someone, then be at the church at 7:10 p.m. and there will be some cars going over.

We are looking forward to a GREAT rehearsal and **M.A.R.S** in the Marcatos' living room that night including some good FUN, FOOD and FELLOWSHIP.

"MARK" your calendars **NOW!**

♪ ♪ ♪ ♪ ♪

4. In each issue of *Choir Notes,* list the entire **Music For The Month** which will be coming up. This organizes you as the director as well as adds professionalism to the entire program. Arrange for all solos, ensembles, instrumentalists, anthems, responses, and other special music for the entire month.

The following is an example:

♪ ♪ ♪ ♪ ♪

Music For September

September 7
Prelude
Prelude and Fugue in c minor — J. S. Bach
Albert E. Bass, Organist

Introit
Let All Mortal Flesh Keep Silence — Gustav Holst

Anthem
O Lord God Of My Salvation — Franz Schubert/
Hines

Prayer Response
Lamb Of God (excerpt) — Mozart/Wilson

Offertory
I Will Arise — Amer. Folk Arr. Susan Byler

Benedictional Response
The Lord Bless You And Keep You — Peter C.
Lutkin

Postlude
Psalm 19 — Benedetto Marcello

September 14
Prelude
Voluntary in C Major — Henry Purcell
Mary Moderato and Paul Pitch, Trumpeters
Albert E. Bass, Organist

Introit
Praise the Lord! — Hal H. Hopson

Anthem
My Shepherd Will Supply My Need — Virgil
Thomson

Call To Prayer
Lead Me, Lord — Samuel Wesley (hymnal)

Offertory
Joy In The Morning — Natalie Sleeth
Brass Ensemble: Mary Moderato, Paul Pitch,
Vince Ventilhorn and Vi Brato

Benedictional Response
Spirit Of The Living God — Daniel Iverson
(hymnal with choir and congregation)

Postlude
Carillon — Louis Vierne

September 21
Prelude
Soul, Adorn Thyself With Gladness — J. Brahms
Albert E. Bass, Organist

Introit
This Is The Day (excerpt) — Angell and Cooper

Anthem
The Old Hundredth Psalm Tune — R. Vaughan
Williams
Mary Moderato, Trumpet descant

Prayer Response
Bless Us This Day (excerpt) — Julie Knowles

Offertory
Alleluia — Randall Thompson

Benedictional Response
Thee We Adore from *The Seven Last Words* —
Theodore Dubois

Postlude
Toccata in e minor — Pachelbel

September 28
Prelude
String Quartet in C (4th movement) — Joseph
Haydn
Victor Violon, Valene Violine, Viola d'Amore and
Vi Cello

Introit
Psalm 150 — John Harper

Anthem
My Eternal King — Jane M. Marshall

Call To Prayer
Turn Your Eyes Upon Jesus — Helen Lemmel
(hymnal)

Offertory
Now Let Every Tongue Adore Thee — J. S. Bach

Benedictional Response
God Be In My Head — John Rutter

Postlude
Cantilena — Rheinberger

♪ ♪ ♪ ♪ ♪

43

You have accomplished three things by listing all of the music for the upcoming month:

1. The work load for the month has been set up for the choir which organizes all concerned with definite goals to work toward in rehearsals.

2. It has been revealed to all of the choir members that they are involved in a well-organized group which does not flounder around during the month trying to decide what should be done.

3. You have given advance notice and recognition to the various individuals who will have a specific solo or ensemble duty to perform during the upcoming month.

This gives good reason as to why music committee meetings, worship committee meetings, and meetings with the church pastor should have an essential purpose in *planning ahead*.

Pray that the Holy Spirit will be at work in your worship services. This listing of music may necessitate some minor changes. Especially, the benedictional response listed may not be the one needed for a particular morning. Recently our pastor preached a sermon that seemed to call out for us to join hands in the congregation for the close of the worship service and sing, "Lord, I Want To Be A Christian In My Heart." This Sunday service ended more effectively than with the choir singing the scheduled "The Lord Bless You And Keep You."

5. Include a column in each issue of *Choir Notes* called **Attendance Percentage For The Month.**

The attendance percentage can be figured from a possible 100 percent for each choir section for the preceding month.

At the end of each month, list the names of the choir members who had perfect attendance at all rehearsals and services for the preceding month. Also, you may want to list the members who missed only one rehearsal or service during the month. This allows you to recognize more members — award more honors if you will — and give some pats on the back.

Always mark a person present if he or she attends any part of the rehearsal or service.

The impressive way it is typed up in the *Choir Notes* can be helpful.

The following is an example:

♪ ♪ ♪ ♪ ♪

Attendance Percentage For March
Perfect attendance for March:
Tam Bourine, Gregory Chant, Polly Choral,
Taran Tella, Al Toclef, Justin Tonation, Virg Tuoso

Basses:	92.6%
Altos:	88.4%
Sopranos:	78.3%
Tenors:	67.9%

Those who missed only one time at either rehearsal or service during the month of March:
Angie Aeolian, Al Legro, Sara Nade, Sam Phonic, Cass Tanets

Average Attendance for March: 29.6 members
Top Attendance Rehearsal for March: 34 on Wed., March 9
Top Attendance Sunday for March: 37 on Sunday, March 23

** Congratulations to all **

♪ ♪ ♪ ♪ ♪

6. A popular feature of each issue of *Choir Notes* is a column that may be called **News About Choir Members And Their Families.**

You may choose to shorten the title. You may want to use this title because it says exactly what it is. Strangely enough, many choir members grab their copy of *Choir Notes*, turn to the back, and read this column first before looking at the beginning of the monthly issue.

Working closely with people, especially in a caring situation, you will learn a lot of news that will be interesting to others.

New grandparents want people to hear about the birth of the cutest, smartest baby that was ever born. Many members from time to time will be presented with awards and honors. Even in the summertime, you may tell an exciting point about a member's vacation trip. Good humor and positive thinking in this column can be good motivational devices.

The column might read something like the following:

♪ ♪ ♪ ♪ ♪

News About Choir Members
And Their Families

I was reminded of "Where Two or Three Are Gathered" when on our trip to Dollywood, I looked up to the top of Daredevil Falls to see three from our choir about to come down that big dip. There was **Mary Major, Mickey Minor,** and **Dee Crescendo** all gathered together. Have you ever heard **Mary** scream? You don't want to hear it ...

Oh, yes, I told you last week that I would tell you something about **Ben Ediction** in the *Choir Notes*. Two weeks ago you may have seen **Ben** run into the choir room breathlessly grabbing for his robe. When I inquired about his haste, **Ben** told me that his car wouldn't start. So, **Ben** and his family had to miss Sunday school as they walked all the way in from Cadence Drive. He simply said, "Well, I told you I would be here." Now, that's dedication ...

Tam and **Tim Pani** were back in choir Sunday morning just having returned from a terrific trip to London, England. Some highlights of the trip were seeing Alec Guinness and hearing the choir at Westminster Abbey ...

Sara Bande has a trip to Hawaii in the planning. I thought she might invite the whole choir, but she hasn't yet ...

Congratulations to **Libby Retto** who will receive her B.A. degree from La Scala University at the commencement exercises on Friday evening. God speed to you, Lib, in your new job at the Guiseppe Green Company. Glad you will still be in town and in the church ...

Art Peggio had a couple of teeth removed. Okay, just so it doesn't hurt your singing, **Art**. We want those notes sung, not whistled ...

♪ ♪ ♪ ♪ ♪

This is the kind of fun you can have in your *Choir Notes* under your column called **News About Choir Members And Their Families.** It gives recognition to many, it gives fun for others to read, and it shows the love and care displayed among the choir members. And, it *motivates*!

Your particular church situation will dictate what type columns to use or omit in your *Choir Notes*. Here are a few more ideas that may be utilized in an interesting and motivating manner:

7. In a column called **From The Mail Box** you may reprint a nice letter received from one of the congregational members expressing appreciation for the music and the choir. Or you might reprint a newsy note received from a past choir member who has moved to another city.

8. Welcome New Members. List the new members' names with some interesting background as to their work, family, hobbies, and past honors. This truly will welcome new members to the choir.

47

9. Your Prez Sez. The president of the choir may have something very special that can be said in each issue of your *Choir Notes*. This is an excellent way to utilize the president's leadership in your communications. Be sure to print the president's name at the end of this column which you may want to call **Your Prez Sez** which, by the way, was suggested by a creative president in our choir.

10. Important Tidbits. You might call these news items **Short Notes** or **Important Notes** or **Final Notes** or how about **Grace Notes!** In this column you can emphasize some important dates, events, or other announcements.

11. Every production needs a **Closing**. Use your own personality as to how you close your monthly issue of *Choir Notes*.

If an example of how I have closed mine will help you, then here it is:

♪ ♪ ♪ ♪ ♪

Well, it's about time to end another issue of *Choir Notes*. I want to thank all of you for your dedicated work. We share and we care ... We play and we pray ... We give and we live ... We cry and we sigh ... We attain and we maintain ... We thank and we prank ... We arrange and we change ... We exchange and we interchange ... We advance and we enhance ... We chant and we descant ... We bring and we sing ... We dare and we care ... We care and declare ... We care about each other ...

Being a Christian is at the top of the mountain for me. Christ changed my life. My only sadness is to see so many around in this world who don't understand what it means. But at least we can touch as many as our own lives can, *and* we can sing it from the chancel at the top of our voices every Sunday.

48

So, until next time let's be sure to ask Christ to dwell in our lives every day and help others to see God through us. Get them to choir practice and we'll all tell them.

And *remember* ...

Ye Ole Wise Cantor says: What a worried, wrinkled Christian needs is a faith lift.

♪ ♪ ♪ ♪ ♪

Have a file in the choir room marked *Choir Notes*. All during the month, drop in this file any items that need to go in the next month's issue. At the beginning of the month, it is very simple to pull out all of the information and sort it for writing the *Choir Notes*.

Enjoy writing and communicating with the choir members each month. It is fun to write as though you are talking personally to each choir member. A lot of the choir members have told me that it is fun to read the *Choir Notes* too.

If it is fun to write them and fun to read them, then we must be *communicating* ... and yes, *motivating*!

> *Let no evil talk come out of your mouths, but only what is useful for building up, as there is need, so that your words may give grace to those who hear.*
> — Ephesians 4:29

8. M.A.R.S.

No, this is not a story about outer-space; however, many choir members on occasion have stated that the M.A.R.S. is "out of this world."

Very simply, **M.A.R.S.** stands for **Monthly After-Rehearsal Social**. It means that once a month the choir has a social following choir rehearsal. But, there is a little more to it than that.

Each month the choir members who have a birthday during that month throw the party for the rest of the choir. That month's birthday people bring the fruit punch and other refreshments. A lot of the fun is to see what new delectable, nutritious, culinary preparations will be brought to spring on our waiting palates.

Let's say that you have just finished a good rehearsal for your upcoming Sunday service. Everyone feels good about the music that you have worked on quite strenuously. Now you can relax and enjoy each other's company in a different setting. Move to the room across the hall for good fun, food, and fellowship!

The birthday people will be scampering around the room getting the ice in the punch bowl and lighting the candles in the table's centerpiece.

The rest will sing "Happy Birthday." Of course, include the names of all those who have a birthday that month. The choir being a musical organization, and since everyone enjoys singing so much, the four-part rendition of "Happy Birthday to You" usually makes very nice music. Someone always says, "Hey, that's good enough to sing at a Sunday service." (Don't laugh! We did it one Sunday to honor a ninety-year-old birthday "girl" in our congregation.)

Every choir probably has a couple of photography buffs who will enjoy taking some candid shots of the people while they move around the table of food. Their finished products in a week or so will keep the **M.A.R.S.** attitude alive. Also, the photos can be displayed on the choir room bulletin boards for a while which will give some continued enjoyment to the members.

The choir's social chairperson may serve as your **M.A.R.S.** coordinator. It is his or her job to be sure that the birthday people for the month know what the other members will be bringing and be certain that everything needed will be present.

If too many members have birthdays one month and not enough another month, it is the social chairperson's job to see about making enough switches to make it work every month. Even this is a motivational device. It gets a lot of people involved.

Once people get involved, refreshments begin to take on interesting patterns. For instance, in one of our choirs we had a Filipino family. When it came their time to help with **M.A.R.S.**, we knew that we would have the privilege of relishing some of their native dishes. In summer months, some of the ladies might suggest chilled fruit dishes and watermelon.

You could have bowls of plain fresh veggies and fruits for those who need to watch their weight and cholesterol. Once when my wife and I returned from a trip to Hawaii, we enjoyed bringing some fresh pineapples to **M.A.R.S.** We cut them and served them to the choir members right on the spot.

Once in a while, a choir member may invite the choir to his or her home for rehearsal and **M.A.R.S.** It works out very well. The choir member needs to have a piano and enough chairs. The director will take a music stand. The librarian will put the rehearsal choir folders in boxes that are just the right size. A couple of the choir members can help unload the boxes at the home and place them by the entrance door. And, voila! You are ready for a good rehearsal.

A rehearsal in a living room can be great. In some rooms the acoustics are wonderful, and the choir members get to sit closer and hear better than in some choir rooms. This sometimes makes for a very good practice.

Following the choir practice, the choir can enjoy a good **M.A.R.S.** in the home.

Yes, **M.A.R.S.** is a social event. But it is a gathering of Christians who have in common a love for music. Sing together, praise the Lord together, minister to others through your music, care about each other, and yes, have fun, food, and fellowship as a group once a month. You can call it **M.A.R.S.** It's out of this world!

> *... I hope to see you soon, and we will talk together face to face. Peace to you. The friends send you their greetings. Greet the friends there, each by name.* — 3 John 14-15

9. Annual Choir Christmas Dinner

All church choirs exert special effort to get the Advent and Christmas music ready for the various services for the season. All Sundays around Christmas take on a great importance, especially the Sunday in Advent preceding Christmas Day. Most churches have special services during the month of December.

This hard work in making beautiful music and singing praises to our Lord during this very inspirational season is quite a motivation for the choir members in itself. In the midst of this excitement, the choir members may find a great deal of enjoyment with their **Annual Choir Christmas Dinner**.

The members in the choir can come up with some creative and innovative ideas. Here are some that have been successful.

Many weeks in advance of the annual dinner, the choir officers select a good night for the event that seems to be suitable. They stand open for invitations to hold this dinner in someone's home. This is really an enlarged M.A.R.S. (Incidentally, no M.A.R.S. is held in December. The Christmas dinner is held in its place.)

The selected date is placed as soon as possible on the official church calendar. The church pastors and other staff members and their guests are invited to this gala.

This is the night that the choir members with their spouses or other guests dress out for the occasion in their Christmas splendor. The home to which the choir is invited usually has the Christmas decorations up which add to the festivities.

Each choir member is asked to bring a covered dish. A sign-up sheet is placed on the choir bulletin board by the social chairperson about two weeks in advance of the dinner. This is so the choir members can sign up if they plan to attend, and can state the number of guests to be invited. In addition, all members designate what food selection they will bring.

The social chairperson coordinates the arrangements making certain that all needed items will be brought. This dinner is inexpensive to each individual, but in the combination of dishes, you can be assured that it will truly be a feast.

Following this delightful dinner on that evening, the social chairperson has made arrangements for a program. This is fun time. On some occasions, inexpensive gifts can be brought by each person. Then the fun goes like this.

Numbers are drawn and the person with the lowest number opens a gift of his or her choosing. The next numbered person opens a gift and can either keep the gift just opened or take the gift that the other person opened. This continues until all gifts are opened. This can be a hilarious night as people on down the line open a gift and may select any opened gift of their choosing.

In your choir, it may be traditional for the choir members to present a gift to the director and the organist. These gifts need not be expensive. The fun you can have is the way in which the choir president makes the presentation. Over the years you will find some choir presidents who are creatively entertaining with the presentations.

The gifts may be wrapped in an odd manner or disguised with a misleading card attached. The directions can be given out where to locate the gifts as a scavenger hunt. The director and organist then will move in and around the house searching for clues as to the next location in the hunt for the gifts.

One year an artistic choir president presented a gift of silver to the director — silver coins, that is! Different size coins were used to designate whole notes, half notes, and quarter notes. The large attractive cardboard "piece of music" formed the notation with coins to "We Wish You A Merry Christmas."

It is no oddity for the program to be centered around music. These people have in common a love of music. They love to sing. A member with a guitar may lead a fun session of Christmas songs. When the final song turns out to be "Amazing Grace," the choir members in beautiful harmony with one another reflect on their real purpose in being. They feel that oneness among themselves and with God. We can praise the Lord with the Annual Choir Christmas Dinner.

For where two or three are gathered in my name,
I am there among them.   — Matthew 18:20

10. A Little Bit Of Broadway

All of us love the beautiful, God-given summertime. It comes around every year, and every year choir directors and choir members get inspired to do things with the choir. Summertime is a time for picnics, softball games, swimming parties, outings, and concerts in the park.

Some summer, this thought may come to your minds:

"Why not have a night this summer when the choir sings a group of Broadway show tunes just for fun?"

Your thoughts continue:

"Look! This group of singers represents some of the most dedicated, loyal, devoted workers in this church. We usually sing two anthems for Sunday worship services, plus the extra specials during the year at Easter, Thanksgiving, Christmas, Founders Day, and more. This means that we sing over a hundred anthems a year not to mention the many introits, benedictional responses, calls to prayer, and other things.

"We have a good musical organization, responsive to good rehearsing, and why not have a fun night and sing completely different things, such as some of the great Broadway musical selections?"

Yes, that's what might come to your thoughts.

You good students of the Gestalt psychology of learning know that this first thought (or synthesis) is bound to be analyzed. After analysis, one arrives at another level of synthesis. Forgive the academic dialogue, but let's say how this initial thought might materialize:

> At first, you were going to have a night of fun with the choir singing some Broadway songs. Then you thought, "In this good, old summertime let's have a watermelon cutting. All of the choir families can come, and we can sit around and sing Broadway songs."

Then, as the choir begins to read through some fun things, you begin to analyze with the thought, "Isn't it a shame that others can't hear and enjoy this?"

So then you decide to have the event following a night of church committee meetings. This way some of the congregation may enjoy staying another hour and hearing the Broadway music.

In final analysis, why not have a night of great Broadway music for the whole church? Some even suggested that the musical night be preceded by a church-wide dinner.

As the time approaches, everybody gets excited. Some want to sing solos, some want to sing in ensembles, and a barbershop quartet is formed for the occasion. An artist in the choir gets inspired to make a long banner to go across the top of the performing area to appear as a marquee on a Broadway theater reading **A Little Bit Of Broadway**.

The publicity leading up to the eventful evening speaks of what is to be, plus the appearance of a special guest artist. Keep the name of the guest artist a secret even from the choir members. It creates a lot of talk and excitement. On the night of the performance, the special guest artist may turn out to be, as in one of our Broadway nights, the church pastor dressed in cowboy attire and singing a western song.

You are fortunate enough to acquire the services of a professional instrumental combo, or an excellent in-church organization, to accompany some of the selections.

So, what started as a fun night with just the choir ends up as a church-wide fun gala!

The date for the Broadway night finally arrives. The choir has a three-hour rehearsal with the band on one night, and does the performance on the next evening.

To say the night is a success has to be a masterpiece of understatement. The following year, the excitement of the past year develops into A Little Bit Of Broadway II. Yes, the year after that you do A Little Bit Of Broadway III.

You may wish to give your night a different name. However, A Little Bit Of Broadway XXI is possible with a name like that.

In doing a Broadway night with your choir, you should consider following certain guidelines. It should be understood that everyone involved will use discretion in the music that is chosen. One has to be careful of some Broadway songs because of the ideas they suggest.

You are able to find a great wealth of beautiful and exciting Broadway musical selections. There are appropriate songs from *The Sound of Music, The Music Man, The Fantasticks, Carousel, The King and I, Les Miserables, Phantom of the Opera, Peter Pan,* and *The Secret Garden* to name a few. There could be no more beautiful words to a Broadway tune than those of "Tomorrow" from *Annie*. Some selections have religious connotations, such as "Climb Every Mountain" from *The Sound Of Music,* "You'll Never Walk Alone" from *Carousel,* and "Bring Him Home" from *Les Miserables*.

You might consider the tradition of ending every Broadway night with the audience participating in singing "God Bless America" by Irving Berlin.

The choir director or whoever is chosen to be the program announcer needs a gimmick. One year you might use different hats to introduce the different numbers. Another year you might introduce the selections with "one-liners" *a la* Henny Youngman.

Also, your comments should remind the audience that you are a church and what your first obligations are. After an exciting number, it would be appropriate to make a comment such as, "Isn't it great that we can come together in our church and have such fun?" Continue to serve the church even in this way.

Toward the end of the program, a comment such as the following could be said: "That song tells about not walking alone. We might try to walk alone, but it won't work. Only when we ask for the Holy Spirit to come into our lives will we come to do the will of God. And that's a good feeling."

Remember, we are to serve the church. There will be some visitors in the audience who love music but have never been invited to understand the closeness of God in their lives. You may be given a golden opportunity to help someone in a spiritual way on your Broadway night.

A Little Bit Of Broadway is not a religious event. There may be those who say it should not be in the church at all. Certainly, this is something you would have to consider in your particular situation.

Here is how you might justify Broadway being done in your church situation:

1. Always have in mind the idea of motivating the choir members to continue to serve in the music ministry of the church. This musical event could help hold their interest.

2. Always have in mind the idea of recruiting new members to serve in the music ministry. Following the Broadway nights in your church, you very likely may recruit new members. When they see how much fun you are having in their church choir, they may want to become a part of it.

3. The audience realizes that they are having fun — fun in their church with their fellow Christians. Their church can have fun and still not lose sight of the purpose of the church as the Body of Christ. People should leave the program with a song in their hearts and a good feeling about their church.

4. Music education is a part of the choir director's job. Musically, the rhythms, harmonies, and rehearsal techniques are very different in singing this style of music. The training that goes into these rehearsals to prepare the Broadway tunes should greatly contribute to the overall musical experience and teaching of the choir members. They should be better prepared to serve in the music ministry for all of the other music.

5. The young people in the church have a place to go and have fun, and they don't have to go beyond their own church. When they see young and old alike having such excitement there, they should have a good feeling about their church.

Finally, this must be said. If all or most of the church were Broadway nights and the like, it would be no good. We in the church cannot take the place of entertainment, television, or Nintendo. The church would soon fold if this were its intention. People could see a better show somewhere else.

What the church has to do is feed people's souls — give the spiritual nourishment for which people search. They need to be led to ask the Holy Spirit to come and dwell in their lives through all decision making, trials, tribulations, and life's problems. This Holy Spirit in our lives is given to us by the grace of God to fulfill our needs and give us peace. This is the purpose of the church.

If Broadway can help lead others into this goal within their church's fellowship, their community, and service and oneness with God, then you might consider A Little Bit Of Broadway.

> *Let mutual love continue. Do not neglect to show*
> *hospitality to strangers, for by doing that some*
> *have entertained angels without knowing it.*
> — Hebrews 13:1-2

11. Making A Professional Recording

"Let's record a cassette album!"

You will be amazed at the excitement that these words can create. If the choir members have pride in their organization, and there are several pieces of music which the choir truly loves and performs well, then everyone will want to share this music through a cassette album.

"Let's record a cassette album" can become a reality. If you properly follow certain steps, you can do a very professional cassette album quite easily.

Recording Sessions

The first step in making a professional recording is the actual recording session or sessions. Your purpose is to get a quality recording on tape.

Depending on your location, you will make a decision as to where the choir will hold the recording sessions. Any situation you choose can be controlled with a little planning. It will need to be quiet.

Most choirs probably will want to record in their own church sanctuary with their own organ rather than go into a recording studio. The finished cassette in an attractive album cover will mean more to you and your congregation if it contains music performed in your usual worshipful environment. The people will hear their choir with their own organ right in their church sanctuary.

There are a number of companies that specialize in doing custom recordings. They bring their equipment into your church and set up for the recording.

It may be advisable to stress the fact that you employ someone with excellent stereo recording equipment. It takes excellent equipment to get an excellent tape. You cannot record on bad equipment with poor microphones and expect the tape to be of high quality.

The choir members will look forward to and thoroughly enjoy the recording session. This will create real excitement. On the night of the recording session, the choir director, organist, and choir members can put all of their attention on the quality of the worshipful, musical performance if a professional sound person has been hired who will attend to all of the technical matters without involving you in the least.

Your choir can be committed on that night to putting your best possible musical qualities on that tape. What is going to be put on that tape is what the people will hear for years to come.

Programming

Good programming is essential at all times. The program that you select for the cassette album needs to be a well-rounded, interesting, effective product that is a complete entity.

You will probably put about five selections on each side of your cassette album. This might include a short introit for the opening of side one, and a choral benediction at the end of side two.

On the album, you will want to contrast your selections. One selection after the other should be in different styles and tempi. Contrast a fast selection with a slow one. Contrast a big, brilliant-sounding anthem with a slower *legato* sound. You do not want two anthems with solos following each other. Separate them.

Before the recording session, give thought as to what selections should be on each side of the tape. Give thought as to what musical selections should follow other contrasting selections on each side.

Copyrights

Some of the selections you will want to record are probably copyrighted compositions. This means that a publisher holds the copyright on the composition or arrangement, and that publisher will be the one to give permission to use the composition in your album. Also, the publishers are to receive royalties.

Many pieces of music are in public domain. This includes the classics (not recently arranged), many hymns, and folk songs. You do not need permission to copy or record songs in public domain.

When recording commercial songs, the copyright laws state that a certain number of cents per song on an album be paid to the publisher or copyright owner. The publisher in turn pays a percentage of this to the composers, authors, and arrangers.

Fortunately, there is an easy way to pay these royalties to the publishers. If you had to write a letter to each publisher and write a separate check for each one, you would have a mountain of paperwork to handle.

So, the Harry Fox Agency was formed to represent all publishers and handle all royalty payments for you. You would need to write a letter to the Harry Fox Agency in New York asking permission to record all of the copyrighted compositions you wish to use.

The Harry Fox Agency office will respond to your request by sending you forms which you will need to fill out and return. You will list one copyrighted composition title per form. The form asks you to state such things as title of composition, composer(s), author(s), arranger, publisher, and exact timing of each selection. You do not send any payment of royalties until your licenses are received.

After your request for recording the pieces has been processed, the Harry Fox Agency will forward to you a bill for the entire royalty payments to all publishers.

From your standpoint, one letter states your request, and one check is mailed to pay the royalties. Then you will be completely through with this aspect of your project, and you can feel good that you handled it in a professional manner.

The address of the Harry Fox office is:

The Harry Fox Agency, Inc.
711 Third Avenue — 8th floor
New York, New York 10017
Telephone: (212) 370-5330

To be specific, at the time of this writing, the cost of the royalties is $.0755 per copyrighted selection for up to five minutes of performing time. After five minutes, the rate per selection is based upon $.0145 per minute or fraction thereof. You would pay these royalties per selection for each cassette made.

In plain arithmetic, if you record four copyrighted pieces (each under five minutes) on which to pay royalties, and you make 200 cassette tapes, then .0755 cents times four copyrights equals .302 cents times the 200 equals $60.40. Your total royalties on the four copyrighted selections for all 200 cassette albums would be exactly $60.40.

Now your recording session is over. You have a beautifully recorded program of music on a stereo tape which you hold in your hand. What do you do now?

Cassette Tapes

Most of you probably will want to make cassette tapes. They can be played at home, in the car, everywhere. You will want to package each cassette tape in an attractive, appealing, inspiring, and professional package.

Many custom recording companies handle the entire process of recording, making cassette tapes, printing, and packaging. Whether that company does it or you handle each step yourself, you should be aware of what is taking place.

Back in the old days when pressing long-play phonograph records was in style, we were concerned with mastering the tape, making plates, pressing the records, and printing large record covers.

Mastering was the process of placing the music from the tape on two album-sized discs. The mastering machine would allow the proper space between the selections to form different bands. These final discs formed the positive album discs on a temporary material.

The two discs were put through a process which created two metal plates — sides 1 and 2 of the record. All of the music was in the grooves on the plates in a negative impression ready for pressing.

These two plates were attached to the machine in the pressing plant which would press or stamp out the records in "hot wax." When the "wax" (really vinyl) cooled, the original tape ended up as a phonograph record.

Some of you may want to use the proper mastering techniques to do a CD album. As mentioned above, probably cassette tapes would be more practical for your church.

A professional company in duplicating your original stereo tape on to cassette tapes will use what is called Dolby. This process helps to keep down any unnecessary noise and produces a good quality finished product.

Tape Liner And Cover

A printed thin cardboard will be packed with each cassette tape which will give the necessary information about the church, choir, and the titles of music on the tape. The tape liner will be folded to serve as the cassette cover.

The information printed on the tape liner should include the name of your choir, name of your church, location, names of the choir director and organist, your pastor's name, and the title of the album if you use one. In addition, you could display a picture of your church, a picture of your choir, or any appropriate and inspirational art work. Also, the word "stereo" should appear on the front of the tape.

On the back of the tape liner, you will want the name of each musical selection with composers, authors, arrangers, publishers, name of performing rights organization (such as ASCAP, BMI, SESAC) if it applies, and the time of performance for each selection.

An example is:

Create in Me a Clean Heart, O God — Carl Mueller ASCAP
G. Schirmer, Inc. 2:15

Also, you may want to list the names of your choir members. This is a good motivational device. You will have space to give a short history of your church. You may want to list the usual activities of the choir. You may want to state a brief "bio" of the director and organist. An inspirational statement is appropriate in presenting your album to your congregation and the public.

You may give the album a name, such as:

The (name of church) Sanctuary Choir
Sings Praises To God

The concluding statement on your album liner may read something like this:

> *The Sanctuary Choir is an all-volunteer choir made up of forty voices. The choir rehearses once a week and sings every Sunday morning for the worship service, as well as on other special occasions including community affairs.*
>
> *The spirit with which the choir members give of their time and talents is reflected in the singing you will hear on this album. A variety of music is represented for the listeners' enjoyment and spiritual enrichment.*
>
> *Even though the Sanctuary Choir is a volunteer choir, all members feel that they are richly rewarded through the joy of witnessing as they sing PRAISES TO GOD.*

A multi-colored tape liner will cost more than a black and white liner. However, you may consider using a colored ink on a different colored cardboard. For instance, maroon ink on a buff cardboard, or blue ink on a different colored cardboard will cost about the same as black ink on white cardboard, but it will give the effect of a multi-colored album liner.

Labels

The labels which go on each side of the tape could have some art work as well as reveal the title of the album, the name of the church, name of the choir, location, and the titles of the selections which appear on each side.

Finally, when the cassette tapes are complete, they are stretch-wrapped in cellophane, and placed in boxes ready for you to take away. Your music is now a cassette album.

When someone said, "Let's record a cassette album," you took on a project to further the professionalism of your music ministry, you helped the attitudes of your choir members, you motivated your people, and you have a product of good, inspirational music which can be heard by ears far removed from your church sanctuary for many years to come.

It showed the congregation and the community that your church is working, moving, ministering, and furthering the Kingdom of God.

> *And he [Jesus] said to them, "Go into all the world and proclaim the good news to the whole creation."*   — Mark 16:15

What Else?

What else may be done to help motivate the volunteers in the music ministry to serve the Lord with gladness, to minister to others, and at the same time find personal spiritual nourishment? What else may be done to make serving in the music ministry of the church exciting, thrilling, an enjoyment, a growing experience, a sharing experience, a sense of service?

12. We Care

"We care" could be a phrase that you often use in your *Choir Notes*. Don't just write it or say it. Do it! When one in your midst has a joy, all are joyful for that person. When one has a burden, all have a burden. Jesus taught us the meaning of love.

At your rehearsal, if someone is reported ill, or a family member is in bad health, your prayer that night should specifically name those people as you are led in prayer. We are promised that where two or three are gathered together in the name of Christ, he will be in our midst.

I recall a personal experience. One night before our choir rehearsal began, the choir room telephone rang. I answered and heard the voice of one of our members who should have been on the way to rehearsal. She told me that she was calling from a hospital room where she was admitted that day. The doctors had found a lump in her breast and she was to go into surgery the next morning,

These were her exact words to me that night on the phone: "I wanted to call and have the choir know that I am in the hospital, because if all of you will pray for me, I know I will be all right."

Do I need to tell you that on that choir rehearsal night, we had our prayer before choir practice started. Every person's caring heart was trained on this child of God missing from our midst that night. Then we began to rehearse.

Our songs of praising God that night made a more inspirational rehearsal than usual. This great rehearsing we did carried over into the next Sunday's worship service. God was in our midst. God should be in the midst of a choir.

Your choir executive committee should formulate a policy of actions to take with regard to people with sickness, in the hospital, and the like. Your committee may wish to formulate a set of rules as they apply to your particular situation.

Here are some guidelines that may help you form your policies:

1. A choir member sick in the hospital could be sent flowers.

2. A member of the immediate family in the hospital could receive a card.

3. A choir member or family member sick at home could be remembered with an appropriate card.

4. A death in the immediate family of a member could prompt your choir secretary to have the church send a memorial card representing your donation of money to the memorial fund of the church in memory of the deceased person.

5. If a choir member dies, you might send flowers or a memorial gift. Of course, the presence of your love would be even greater by attending to the physical needs of the family.

6. You will have occasions of weddings and graduations. Here, too, the secretary may be instructed to send a gift.

We care! This can do a lot in bringing the love of God to human lives.

> *That there may be no dissension within the body, but the members may have the same care for one another. If one member suffers, all suffer together with it; if one member is honored, all rejoice together with it.* — 1 Corinthians 12:25-26

13. Personal Contact

All choir members need that social personal contact. It is not too difficult or time-consuming to send a church bulletin to each choir member who misses a couple of rehearsals or Sunday worship services.

Take a few minutes on Sunday afternoon to write a note on the back of the Sunday's bulletin and mail it to each choir member whom you have missed in choir a couple of times.

This action will let those members know that they were missed, that they are important, that we care about them and hope they are not ill. And it lets them have a copy of that Sunday's church bulletin that they did not get to see. Try it!

A personal contact by telephone or in person is needed when choir members miss more than twice. You will want to inquire if the church can be of any help to them due to some conflict or problem.

Just as the pastor-shepherd looks after the flock in the church, the choir director-shepherd looks after the flock in the choir.

> *Where there is no guidance, a nation falls, but in*
> *an abundance of counselors there is safety.*
> — Proverbs 11:14

14. Membership Involvement

Special talents and skills of the choir members may be utilized which will get members involved.

The choir director will want to assign singers their seats in the rehearsal room as well as the church choir loft in order to achieve the best possible vocal sound. For instance, those singers who read music can be placed among the non-readers to reinforce the sound and the singers' confidence.

The seating should be worked out on paper. You might want to use a small card for each singer so that you can rearrange the cards into the order you wish for them to sit.

Then turn this chart over to a responsible choir member who will be in charge of lining up the choir members to process down the center aisle, or enter the choir loft by way of the side door, or whatever your physical arrangement for entering may be. The choir needs to enter in an orderly and disciplined manner.

If you have an artist in your choir, that person can do various pieces of art work for many causes. This might vary from cartoons for the church newsletter to the heading of *Choir Notes*, layouts for choir programs, posters, and items for special occasions.

If you ever need to renovate the choir room, many talents can be used from laying the carpet to putting in acoustical tile to hanging pictures and chalk boards.

Talented carpenters and woodwork people can build beautiful new choir robe closets, shelving for storage, cases for choir rehearsal and performance folders, and wall platforms for the stereo speakers.

This work would amount to hundreds of dollars if you had to hire companies to do the work. Instead, you can buy the materials and your choir members will not only do the work, but I have found that they will do it cheerfully. The choir can have some nights of good times when the women and men experience a really good feeling in the work they are doing and in their service to the church. For months people will be brought around to see their handiwork.

Try giving your members the opportunity to serve and become involved.

> *Let us then pursue what makes for peace and for mutual upbuilding.* — Romans 14:19

15. Discipline

"My choir is an all-volunteer choir! I can't get rough with them about their talking," said the church choir director to me loudly over the thunderous din in a room which was not acoustically treated.

I was visiting a friend's church choir rehearsal. I tried to keep a smile on my face. Even that became impossible when a choir member began to play rhythms loudly on a metal cabinet in the back of the room. This happened right in the middle of an important musical suggestion by the choir director.

By the way, this particular choral director is one of the best musicians I know with regard to explaining good musical interpretation, styling, phrasing, use of dynamics, and singing expressively. But what good is it? The choir members can't hear a word that he says!

Now let's go visit another church choir rehearsal. This choral director prides himself on "good discipline." This choir director never smiles. If anyone else in his group acts like he or she may smile and say something, the choir director glares at this lowly member with disdain. For a choir member to be relaxed and have a creative thought would be unheard of, because this director's choir room has to be so silent that one could hear a stole from a choir robe drop to the floor.

Yes, this second choir director prides himself on excellent discipline. As I stood there, I couldn't help but wonder, "But is he proud that he has only thirteen members in his choir? And some of them look disinterested."

Somewhere between these two music directors, there has to be a situation that allows for self-expression, creativity from the members, real fun, joy, happiness, and respect for the organization and the church program. At the same time they can have an extremely good environment for a very musical and worshipful rehearsal.

Every director has a unique personality and has to operate according to what works for him or her. It would be very difficult to follow the pattern that someone else uses.

However, any musical director of a group should consider *firmness* in his or her leadership. A certain quality or standard should be established. An attitude of firmness as well as *fairness* should be used to attain and not deviate from that desired quality or standard. The leader should be *consistent* in attaining the right attitudes toward achieving the desired goals.

We need to keep several other things in mind. If a choir rehearsal is in utter chaos, there will be a number of members who will be turned off. They will see no organization. They will see a sloppily prepared choir, because they can't hear the good suggestions and teaching by the director. The choir members can't execute the musical suggestions by the director with the sense of wanting to do well.

The choir members in an undisciplined choir can have no respect for the organization. Some of the singers will want to sing musically with good tone quality, good intonation, precise phrasing, good attacks, releases, and musical interpretation. Some of the students will want to learn. These choir members will be lost. Probably they will drop out of the choir program, all because of poor discipline.

In a situation like this, the director's talents are wasted, the choir members' talents are not being utilized to the fullest, and the church music program that could be functioning well with high spirits is failing to operate at an effective standard of serving the church spiritually.

When conducting, some choir directors stand on the floor on the same level as the singers. Every choir room needs a director's podium. The director doesn't stand on a podium in order to "look down on the singers!" (Now, that's a bad joke!)

There are at least four good reasons for the director's using a podium:

1. By having to look up, the choir members will be able to see the director and will be able to follow the director's conducting.

2. This will make the singers sit up straight since they are having to look up. This posture will help them with proper breathing which will aid good tone production and good vocal control.

3. The director can hear the whole group better by being up above the choir rather than standing on the same level as the singers in front of just one section.

4. This simple podium structure in your rehearsal room aids the choir members' attitudes in realizing that you are operating a professional program. Choir members want to be part of something that is good and professionally operated.

Always help your choir members feel that each person is a member of a well-organized group — a group that they can respect as well as feel respected by. Church musicians want to be members of a group in which they feel that they are arriving at a high standard of achievement and fulfilling their goal of serving the spiritual nourishment of the church members.

Church choral directors through the music program are in a position to help young people feel wanted and loved. We can help them socially and raise their self-esteem. A bad "discipline problem" is probably just young people who are angry because they don't feel that anyone will listen to them and think that they are important. Remember, they don't care how much you know until they know how much you care!

The choir members must know that they are a part of a body that has definite goals. Learning and interpreting good music is a goal that can bring much happiness and inspiration to the musicians forever. This standard of quality will serve as Godly inspiration to the listeners.

> *But all things should be done decently and in*
> *order.*   — 1 Corinthians 14:40

16. Choir Children

We read in Proverbs, "Train children in the right way, and when old, they will not stray" (Proverbs 22:6).

We were in the grocery store and my daughter said, "Look, there is Mike Marcato." I have to admit that he had grown so much that I did not recognize him at first. My daughter explained that they used to play together at the church on choir practice nights.

The children of the choir members should be welcome on choir practice nights. You might consider paying a person to sit with choir children. This permits their parents to come to choir practice.

At the same time, the children have fun in their church utilizing the various materials in the rooms. They have a good time. They look forward to coming to the church on these nights. They have a good feeling about their church. They should grow up with good memories.

Choir children are important to us. And, oh yes, on the night of M.A.R.S., "Come on up, kids, and have some punch."

> *But as for you, continue in what you have learned and firmly believed, knowing from whom you learned it and how from childhood you have known the sacred writings that are able to instruct you for salvation through faith in Christ Jesus.*
> — 2 Timothy 3:14-15

How Lovely are the Messengers

Anthem for Mixed Chorus

Rom. v: 15,16

F. Mendelssohn

17. Cantatas

There are many occasions when cantatas or oratorios are rehearsed and performed on a planned schedule. Many church choirs perform a cantata at Christmas time and at Easter.

Have you ever put a cantata or oratorio in your rehearsal folders just to work on at spare times with no definite schedule that you have to meet?

There are some months during the year when you do not have Palm Sunday, Easter, Pentecost, Founders' Day, All Saints' Day, Thanksgiving, Advent, and Christmas for which to plan music.

A choir should have at all times some project or goal to be working toward. During the slack months, work on your unscheduled cantata or oratorio.

Finally, you will arrive at a time when you realize that the music is taking shape, and you can schedule a good time to present the work to the church and community.

> ... *I will proclaim your name to my brothers and sisters, in the midst of the congregation I will praise you.* — Hebrews 2:12

The musical composition below can be effective as a Choral Call To Worship (Introit), or a Prayer Response, or a Benedictional Response.

God's Mercy Endureth

Ellis D. Thompson

God's mer - cy en - dur - eth, God's mer - cy en - dur - eth, Praise to God! A - men. A - men. A - men.

(The publisher grants permission for you to make multiple copies of this choral response for use in your church choir.)

86

18. Special Arrangements And Compositions

Many well trained choir directors try their hand at composing and arranging. One can enjoy contributing a great deal of special music which the choir can rehearse and perform.

Special arrangements make a choir unique. The choir can present to the congregation music which has never been heard before by anyone. This makes the choir something special. The choir members realize what a unique contribution they are making to the worship services.

It is relatively easy for one to write original introits and benedictional responses. These begin and end a worship service with a really special sound and message that has not been heard before.

One might write original compositions as well as arrangements of hymn tunes. Sometimes the music can be done with organ, sometimes *a cappella*, and sometimes with orchestra. Doing these new pieces does a lot for the congregation and the worship services. They create a lot of excitement for the choir members as they prepare them.

In one of my choirs, we had a member who was a professional composer. He composed and arranged a series of poems giving various choir members solo parts. It was exceptionally fine music — fine writing — and was a project worth doing for our church.

Keep in mind that you cannot arrange a song which is copyrighted without receiving permission from the copyright holder. In most cases, this is quite easily obtained. Any song which is PD (in public domain) can be arranged with no permission needed. Many hymns in your hymnal are PD. Giving a special touch to anything, such as a new arrangement, makes a difference and creates interest.

Your church may be interested in having an original hymn com-position contest. The contest should be open to everyone in the church. Some church members may enter words only. Some may enter music only. Some may write both words and music.

The hymn which is judged first place winner in the hymn con-test should then be written in a four-part harmonization so it can be sung by the choir.

Publicize the contest to the extent that many will get involved in some way. The end result will be something creative, inspiring, a new piece of music, renewed interest in the choir program and the church — and *motivation*.

> *Praise the Lord! Sing to the Lord a new song, his praise in the assembly of the faithful.*
>
> — Psalm 149:1

19. Composition Contest

A song-writing contest can create interest in your church. You can establish good motivational interest within the choir members as well as the entire congregation.

Good planning can achieve excellent results with this composition contest project.

A composition contest committee should be set up. The committee in charge would need to establish some guidelines in order to make the contest fair and so you don't run into an obstacle after it is too late to explain a rule gracefully.

The following outline may be of some help to you as your committee begins to think out what would be effective for your church members in your particular situation.

Entries may be submitted in three categories:

1. Hymn: Entries are to be in hymn form. Words or music or both may be entered. The words should be more than one stanza. The hymn should be no longer than 32 measures of music. It is suggested that contestants consult the hymnal for form and length. A home recording of the hymn may be entered.

2. Contemporary Christian Song: Entries may be submitted in lead sheet form complete with melody, lyrics, and chord symbols or with piano accompaniment. Contestants may submit only words or only music. A recording of the song is an acceptable entry.

3. Traditional Church Solo: Entries may be submitted as either words or music. An entry may be in lead sheet form or written with melody, lyrics, and keyboard accompaniment. A recording may be submitted as the entry.

A definite time should be set regarding:

1. The amount of publicity and information you wish to present to the church congregation before the deadline for entries.
2. An exact deadline for entries.
3. Judges to be chosen and publicized. Judges could include the choir director, organist, choir president, and possibly a music teacher who is a member of the congregation.
4. The exact date as to announcing the winners.
5. The time element to be allowed to arrange the music if needed, and ample rehearsal time to prepare the selection to be performed.

Contest Guidelines:

1. All music must be clearly written on music manuscript paper if entered in notation.
2. The entry could be submitted as a home cassette recording.
3. All lyrics submitted must be type written.
4. A contestant must submit four legible copies of the original or four tape recordings. The contestant should keep the original.
5. Include no name of contestant on the entry copies, but print name and address on the outside of the envelope.
6. The choir secretary will open all entries and assign a number to each entry. The judges will have only a number to go by for each entry.
7. All lyrics and music must be original except for the use of scriptural passages.
8. Entries may be a collaboration effort by two or more people.
9. No entries are to have been previously performed in public or published.
10. Mail or bring all entries to: (state exact address).

If any questions arise concerning the entry rules, the contest committee should meet, make a judgment, and then publicize the answer to all contestants prior to the entry deadline.

What a great Sunday morning worship service when the choir or soloists sing the winning songs in each category. At that worship service, you can truly "sing unto the Lord a new song."

As you sing psalms and hymns and spiritual songs among yourselves, singing and making melody to the Lord in your hearts.   — Ephesians 5:19

TRUMPETS

WITH CONGREGATION

Christ the Lord is risen to- day, — Al- le- lu- ia!

All on earth and an- gels say,— Al- le- lu- ia!

20. Using Instrumental Music

Many choirs add instruments to some of their music. This helps to involve more people. Many players of instruments often want an opportunity to play.

The use of instruments can be as simple as a solo or duet playing the prelude, to a brass ensemble playing with the hymns, to a string quartet playing with the anthem. If you have enough people in your church who play instruments, you may form an orchestra to accompany various choir selections.

Orchestra

You may be fortunate to have enough instrumentalists in your church to form what you might call a Chamber Orchestra. Your church probably would not have members enough to support a full symphonic instrumentation. However, this could offer an opportunity to invite some other community players into your church.

The instruments in a standard orchestra would involve woodwinds, brass, strings, and percussion. The basic woodwinds would be flutes, oboes, clarinets, and bassoons. Brass instruments would involve french horns, trumpets, trombones, and tuba. The string section has violins, violas, 'cellos, and string basses. Percussion instruments involve tympani, other drums, cymbals, and more.

It is possible to form almost any combination of instruments and make very impressive music.

Many orchestrations may be purchased from the classical and traditional repertory to be played by a small group. Also, some music publishers publish orchestra parts with their choral publications. Some music can be written specifically for the group.

Handbells

The handbell choir is a very big part of many church music programs. Several handbell choirs may be formed for a variety of groups and ages.

Performing with handbells requires a special amount of training in order to teach and properly direct the groups. However, instruction is easily obtained. Many colleges offer a summer course in handbell directing. The Choristers Guild often offers a seminar in handbells. Many church conferences and summer camps offer training.

A church choir director who is beginning a handbell program might contact another choir director in the area who has a well organized handbell choir program. He or she can give specific information as to where you may obtain a good set of handbells, other necessary equipment, and a good start on selecting music.

Recruiting your congregational members to play handbells is a very easy job. Bells are fun to play, and the sound is beautiful even when played by beginners. Your church situation may have an elementary handbell choir, a youth handbell choir, and an adult handbell choir meeting at different rehearsal times.

David also commanded the chiefs of the Levites to appoint their kindred as the singers to play on musical instruments, on harps and lyres and cymbals, to raise loud sounds of joy.
— 1 Chronicles 15:16

21. Stereo Equipment

Fine stereo equipment in your choir room can become a reality more easily than you think. A little research can allow you to purchase excellent sound equipment at a price that you can afford.

Your music program should benefit by having eight pieces of equipment for the choir room. Most choir rooms still have a turntable for records since there are so many valuable albums in the music libraries. You will need a stereo receiver, a compact disc player, two stereo speakers, a cassette tape deck, and two microphones. This should give you all that you need to do a very efficient job.

Your choirs need to hear recordings of the music that you are doing. Especially with your children and youth choirs, you may have a lot of great orchestral accompaniments for some of the music you are doing.

With good sound equipment, you can set the volume in the speakers to the same level of the choir and have the choir sing right along with the recording. This will speed up the learning of new music when you need to learn quickly. Have the choir sing along with the entire composition coming out of the speakers. This is a real course in speed learning. This can be used in combination with your usual techniques in teaching music reading.

If your music department is interested in acquiring some good sound equipment, the series of events might be planned as the following:

The announcement should be made to the church that the music ministry wants to obtain stereo sound equipment for the choir room. Also, an explanation should be given as to its needs, its purposes, its uses, and its benefits to the church program. You might be amazed as to how people begin to make donations. Many should want to have a part in this project.

Consult with members of the choir and possibly others who have some knowledge of sound equipment. Do a great deal of research into different units, prices, and what you think will fit into your particular needs in your particular architectural environment. The end result should be the purchase of some excellent equipment.

After you have the equipment, the choir and church will be proud of its quality. This may even prompt a carpenter in your congregation to build small platforms on the wall for the stereo speakers.

Place the speakers on the wall, one on each side of the choir room. Place them the proper distance apart by experimenting at various distances so that the best possible stereo acoustical effect is obtained.

You can patch (wire) your equipment into the receiver so that a big stereo sound will resonate with glory out of the wall speakers. Then you will be able to play records, compact discs, and cassette tapes. With two microphones you will be able to record the choir in rehearsal and play back the choir's work through the speakers.

You should find many uses for your sound equipment in improving the effectiveness of your music ministry. Rehearsal techniques can be adapted to faster learning when it is needed. It will hold the singers' interest. The quality standard will go up since the choirs will have a closer understanding of their performing. The choirs will have a greater pride in the professionalism of the music program.

Yes, even some well chosen sound equipment can be a motivation for the members in the music ministry.

Make a joyful noise to the Lord, all the earth.
Worship the Lord with gladness; come into his
presence with singing.   — Psalm 100:12

22. Musicianship

Most choir members are not music majors or even music students in school. However, most people who love music and love to sing are very interested in learning more about music. It is not unusual for some choir members to enroll in a night adult education music appreciation class. The choir director can further their thirst for knowledge about music.

A choir director should not try to talk down to the choir members. In the course of choir rehearsals, the director should freely use musical terms expecting the singers to learn what is being spoken musically.

A choir director should expect the choir members to know what is meant when a *crescendo* is called for in the music. Dynamic markings should be understood when called by their correct name, such as *piano, pianissimo, forte, mezzo forte,* and *fortissimo.*

In the midst of a rehearsal is when musical terms can be learned by actual usage. The choir members do not have to memorize what *decrescendo* means. They will sit there and rehearse a *decrescendo* in a passage of music giving the appropriate musical interpretation with enough repeats that *decrescendo* will be just a part of the rehearsal vocabulary.

Likewise, other musical terms and ideas will be rehearsed and learned, such as *ritardando, a tempo, accelerando, coda, da capo, legato, rubato, modulation,* and tempi markings such as *allegro, adagio,* and *moderato,* to mention a few.

As choir director, expect your choir members to become better musicians. They want to be better musicians and will take more and more interest in the musical organization of which they take pride in being a member. Musicianship! Choir is a musical learning experience.

The choir director should be very strong in what we call music theory. How else can the director know how to fit notes into the correct chord, know the right harmonic progression, understand a modulation that may occur, know the correct intervals, know which note in the triad should be doubled, know what note of a chord may be omitted, know musical forms, know how certain thematic figures need to be imitated from one choir section to the other, not to mention a complete understanding of and ability to perform all rhythms. With a director who is proficient in music theory, the choir members will begin to learn and understand more.

In recruiting, the director might say to prospects, "You don't have to know how to read music to sing in the choir; but you might be amazed as to how much you end up learning along the way."

You might find that a short story with a punch line thrown in during rehearsal can create some interest — *a la* music appreciation class! For instance:

When working on music by **Felix Mendelssohn** (1809-1847) you might be able to create some interest among the choir members. Make the music come alive by making the singers know more about the composer. Actually, Mendelssohn was a man who lived well. In fact, he was somewhat of a well-to-do, educated aristocrat. His grandfather was Moses Mendelssohn, a Jewish philosopher. (His family was converted to the Protestant faith when Felix was still a child.)

Mendelssohn's father was a banker who loved art. His mother read Homer in the original. It is no wonder that the music of Mendelssohn reflects this highly educated, dignified, aristocratic attitude.

By knowing a few things about the composer, your choir members have a handle to hold on to when singing their music.

Mendelssohn was much loved in England. The first edition of the British *Grove's Dictionary of Music* in 1880, which has been the musical bible for music students, devoted its longest article to Felix Mendelssohn — 68 pages. Bach received eight!

♪ ♪ ♪ ♪ ♪

In some contemporary music that is quite dissonant, there is often a figure or phrase that is used as an "effect" rather than needing the actual harmonic progression. Even in John Stainer's

Crucifixion, which is less dissonant than many works, you might have the choir perform the text, "crucify, crucify ..." in "The Appeal of the Crucified," as a mob shouting rather than have them sing the actual pitches. This gives an "effect" rather than singing the written harmony.

When you perform this work, the choir may enjoy hearing this story about **Igor Stravinsky** (1882-1971), who was on the podium before a school orchestra rehearsing one of his masterful works. As you know, his music is quite difficult to sight read, as his meter changes at every measure at times.

As the orchestra continued rehearsing, one of the double bass players mustered up enough courage to raise his hand to speak. When Stravinsky recognized him the student said, "Maestro, this passage is just impossible for me to play exactly as written at this tempo." A professional orchestra member could play the figure exactly as written. But Stravinsky in his kindness toward this student allowed a big, broad smile to come over his face as he said, "But the sound you are getting as you try to play it is exactly the effect that I want."

♪ ♪ ♪ ♪ ♪

When you work on a piece by Tchaikovsky, you may make the music come alive by telling of his visit to America.

Peter Ilyich Tchaikovsky (1840-1893) is recorded as writing an interesting letter from New York in 1891 when he was invited to the opening ceremonies of Carnegie Hall.

Tchaikovsky wrote:

> "These Americans strike me as very remarkable. In this country the honesty, sincerity, generosity, cordiality, and readiness to help you without a second thought are extremely pleasant.... The houses downtown are simply colossal. I cannot understand how anyone can live on the thirteenth floor. I went out on the roof of one such house. The view was splendid, but I felt quite giddy when I looked down on Broadway.... I am convinced that I am ten times more famous in America than in Europe."

♪ ♪ ♪ ♪ ♪

The Messiah, written by **George Frideric Handel** (1685-1759), lasts about two and a half hours and was composed in just 24 days. Handel wrote it before going to Ireland where a concert hall was being dedicated by performances of his works. Normally, the concert hall held 600 people; but to increase the capacity, women were asked not to wear hoop-skirts, and men were asked to leave their swords at home.

♪ ♪ ♪ ♪ ♪

Johann Sebastian Bach (1685-1750) was a deeply religious man. At the beginning of each sacred composition he wrote the letters J.J. for *Jesu Juva* (Jesus help) and at the end he put S.D.G. for *Soli Deo Gloria* (to God alone the glory.)

A year before his death in 1750, Bach was almost blind. His last composition was the organ piece, "Before Thy Throne I Step, O Lord." He had to dictate it to his son. The piece breaks off before the end, as though death had kept him from finishing it.

Bach's music was largely forgotten for years after his death. But a few composers of the following generations knew some of his compositions and were aware of his genius. For instance, in 1829, Felix Mendelssohn performed the *Saint Matthew Passion,* and Bach's music and his religious fervor have been a regular diet of every serious musician since then.

Bach once said, "The aim and final reason of all music should be nothing else but the Glory of God and the refreshment of the spirit."

Our present choir members who keep this quote with them are bound to sing Bach with a deep feeling and understanding of God's Glory in music.

♪ ♪ ♪ ♪ ♪

Wolfgang Amadeus Mozart (1756-1791) has to be considered one of the most amazing child prodigies in history. By the age of six he could play the harpsichord and violin. He was able to improvise fugues, write minuets, and read music perfectly at first sight. At age eight he wrote a symphony. At age eleven he wrote an oratorio. At age twelve he wrote an opera.

The story is told that at age fourteen, Mozart was in Rome during Holy Week at which time he went to the Sistine Chapel to hear the famous choir perform an unpublished work which was its own treasured property. It was said that anyone caught copying this choral piece was to be punished by ex-communication.

Mozart heard the piece one time. He wrote it out afterward completely. He returned to the chapel with his manuscript to make a few additions and was caught — caught in what was considered a crime. But the fact that Mozart should hear and remember it was so incredible that he not only escaped punishment, but was knighted by the Pope for his musical accomplishments.

In 1791 Mozart's health grew worse. He was working on a Requiem, a Mass for the Dead. Mozart rushed to finish it while on his deathbed. He died shortly before his thirty-sixth birthday, and the final sections of the Requiem are not his. The work was completed from his sketches by his favorite pupil, Sussmayr.

In view of his debts, Mozart received a pauper's funeral. His friends followed the hearse to his funeral, but when a violent storm came upon them, they turned back, leaving the hearse to proceed alone. With not a note of music, Mozart was placed in the common pauper's grave.

♪ ♪ ♪ ♪ ♪

Johannes Brahms (1833-1897) was a romantic who brought a uniqueness to classical forms. For several years Brahms conducted a Viennese musical society which allowed him the vehicle to perform many forgotten masterpieces of Bach, Handel, and Mozart. Brahms had a fine knowledge of older music.

Once after a violinist played a piece by Bach, Brahms was so overcome with its greatness that he took his own music in his hand and threw it to the floor shouting, "After that, how could anyone play such stuff as this!" We think of that as such a strange statement coming from one of the greatest masters of all time.

In truth, Brahms was a loving, tender, compassionate human being. His music proves this. However, he was sometimes feared for his caustic wit.

To a musician who was fishing for compliments, Brahms remarked, "Yes, you have talent. But very little!"

The dear little old ladies whom Brahms was helping in a rehearsal of *The Creation* were admonished, "Why do you drag the tempo so? Surely you took this much faster under Haydn."

When a string quartet played one of his works, the viola player asked Brahms if he was satisfied with the tempo. Brahms snapped back, "Yes, especially yours!"

♪ ♪ ♪ ♪ ♪

There is a marvelous story about the great opera composer, **Giuseppe Verdi** (1813-1901). Verdi disliked hand organs with a passion because most of the time they sounded out of tune, and worst of all, when the person turning the handle would get tired, the tempo would slow down. If there was anything that Verdi couldn't stand, it was out of tune, tired tempo music.

When Verdi died, 300 hand organs were found stored in his basement. He had purchased them and hidden them away in a one-man crusade to rid the world of hand organs!

According to a biographer, Verdi was walking down the street one day when he came upon a dowdy, seedy-looking organ grinder doing his thing, with a flea-bitten monkey holding a tin cup. As Verdi passed by he tapped the organ grinder vigorously on the shoulder, saying, "The tempo! Pick it up, pick it up!" Then he continued down the street holding his hands over his ears.

A few days later, Verdi happened upon the same organ grinder, but with a whole new look. He was wearing a new suit. The organ was polished. The monkey had been given a bath and looked healthy and happy. As Verdi moved closer to the two, he saw a big sign that the man had attached to the organ. It read: "Master musician. Studied with Verdi."

Sometimes you might use this story in a devotional. All of us need to "pick up the tempo" in our spiritual journey and be "touched by the Master!"

♪ ♪ ♪ ♪ ♪

Many people sing the music of **Franz Schubert** (1797-1828) and think that he existed so very long ago. They might feel that his music is so old that they really can't relate to it.

The music is not so old when you realize that Schubert was born after the American Revolution was fought and the Declaration of Independence was signed. During his lifetime, Fulton invented the steamboat, the first steamship crossed the Atlantic, and the Monroe Doctrine was signed. Some who lived at the same time as Schubert were Edgar Allan Poe, Charles Dickens, Robert Browning, and Stephen Foster. No, don't look upon Schubert's music as "that ancient music."

♪ ♪ ♪ ♪ ♪

The story is told about **Ludwig van Beethoven** (1770-1827) who was very hard to get out of bed in the morning. It is told that someone would go to the keyboard and loudly play a I (tonic) chord followed by a IV (sub-dominant) chord followed by a V7 (dominant 7th) chord, and then walk away from the keyboard. Beethoven was forced to scurry out of bed, go the keyboard, and resolve the progressions with a final I (tonic) chord.

By the way, after demonstrating this to your choir, from then on you can expect the choir members to know the sound and the function of a dominant seventh chord!

> *... I will pray with the spirit, but I will pray with the mind also; I will sing praise with the spirit, but I will sing praise with the mind also.*
> — 1 Corinthians 14:15

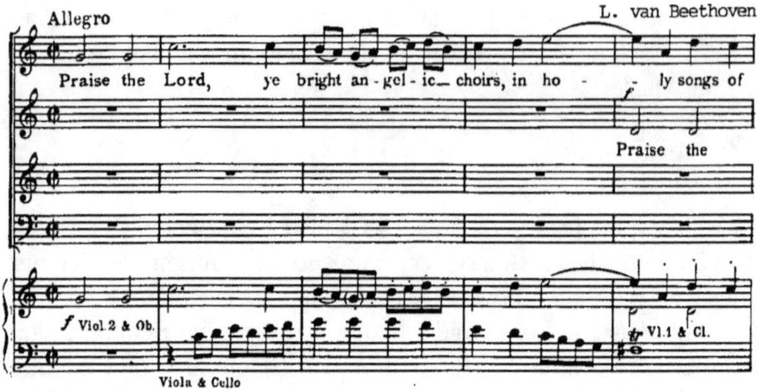

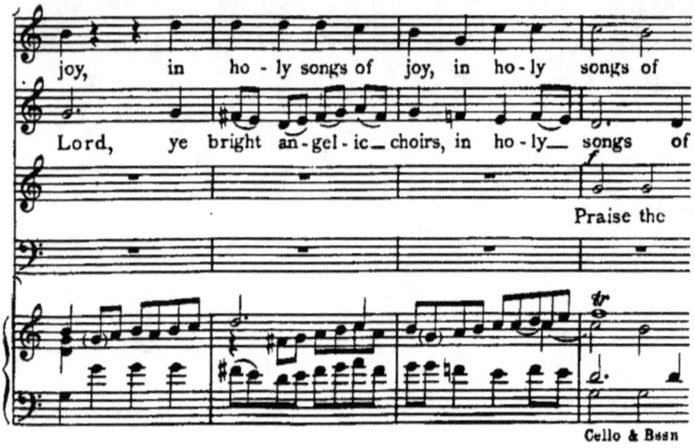

V^7
SOUND
AND
FUNCTION ! !

Conclusion

There are 22 topics that I took up with the class of church music students who came to visit our choir program on that day.

The theme for their field trip was The Motivation Of Choir Members In A Church Music Program. I hope that I gave them some new ideas. I hope that I created some interest with regard to how they may want to set up their choir programs. I hope that they understood that getting people to serve in the choir is not enough. Their recruits have to be motivated to continue to serve.

I remember the last student to leave my choir room on that day. I remember him for the intelligent questions that he asked during my time with the class. Upon leaving the choir room, he thanked me very much for my help, and then he said:

"Mr. Thompson, to sum up this study we could say that motivation will be greatly enhanced by forming a well-organized program, making it interesting and meaningful to the participants, having a caring attitude, and having it guided by good musical and spiritual leadership."

I think he just about said it!

Therefore, my beloved, be steadfast, immovable,
always excelling in the work of the Lord, because
you know that in the Lord your labor is not in vain.
— 1 Corinthians 15:58

Twofold Amen

A - men, A - men.

(The publisher grants permission for you to make multiple copies
of this choral Prayer Response for use with your church choir.)

Appendix

♪   ♪   ♪

Notes From The Choir Director
(Numbers 1-20)

♪   ♪   ♪

♪ A "Note" From The Choir Director ♪

My family received a visit from a member of a congregation I once served. It was a small church, but we had a very nice choir. This dear friend told us that since we left, there had been four or five different choir directors come and go. She seemed to express in her voice much discouragement about the effectiveness of their choir program.

This saddened me very much as I thought back on our days there, and all of the things that took place. I remember how hard all of us worked on so many special worship services, especially the unique and inspiring Easter and Christmas programs.

As my mind drifted back over some memories, I remember when this dear lady came and joined the choir. She had a nice voice and she seemed interested in learning more about music.

She was in the choir for many months, and then one day she said something to me that made me know that the music ministry in the church is all well worth the effort.

She said, "I used to just sing words without really knowing what I was saying. But I remember when we sang something where the actual words of Jesus were spoken in the anthem."

She continued, "I cried as I sang those words. Since then I have paid close attention to the words I sing, and I have felt so very close to God."

I turned quickly so she couldn't see the tears well up in my eyes. It is simply that the Holy Spirit had touched her life. I feel that the church music program played a role in strengthening her spiritual life.

So you can see that I believe in the music ministry in the church. If it only helps ONE, it is worth it.

♪ A "Note" From The Choir Director ♪

One morning a while back, when I woke up, I knew that I had a day before me which was to have problems and would be very difficult for me. It is not good to arise in the morning and be filled with anxiety about that day to come.

This particular morning I got up from kneeling and praying by my bed and walked straight to my table where I keep my billfold, watch, and other items to go in my pockets.

On top of my things I found a piece of paper. I didn't know from where it had come. I later learned that my sister had given my wife the title of a song which she had heard and liked, and thought that I might be interested in getting for the choir.

This is what the piece of paper said: "I Cast All My Cares Upon You." It was simply the title of a song. But in my fearful, anxious feelings of what I had to overcome that day, it was a direct message to me. I didn't know until later why it was there and that it was a song title by Kelly Willard which was published in 1984 by Word Music. I do know that the message carried me through the day.

When I was in the Army during World War II, I always read several verses from my Bible when I got up in the morning. Several months passed, and one of the roughest and toughest guys in my outfit told me, "Tennessee, I know what you do every morning. I wish I had a way I could start my day like that."

Don't think for one minute that what we do doesn't influence the lives of others. Don't think for one minute that what we say, think, and pray about doesn't influence the lives of others. And don't think for one minute that the music we work on and present in worship doesn't help influence the lives of others. It was a song title alone which changed my day!

Please! Let us continue, go forward, and help the power of God's Spirit work through us in bringing light into the lives of others through our music ministry.

♪ A "Note" From The Choir Director ♪

I am glad that our church choir was asked to participate in two recent funerals of our beloved members. I am glad that we could serve our people in this way.

Also, may I express my appreciation to each of you who were able to leave your homes or work areas and form a very nice choir on those two occasions.

The last funeral in our sanctuary was very meaningful to me. The family requested that one of our selections be "Turn Your Eyes Upon Jesus." Your voices blended so well, and your words were sung so clearly and beautifully. Everyone in the sanctuary had to hear every word of that hymn. And, the words touched each heart I am sure.

May we always think of funeral services as being memorial services for our loved ones.

A funeral should not be held to mourn death. Of course, it is a time when we, the deceased one's friends, reveal our grief and sadness that we shall no longer have that loved on in our presence. But, we can be happy that a funeral is a memorial to the life of our deceased loved one who has moved on to live in eternal peace with our Lord.

We can learn from the wonderful jazz tradition which is still practiced today in New Orleans. The great Louis Armstrong and others, on their procession to a funeral, played and sang songs which expressed the grief for their loved one departing from their presence on earth. But, following the service they played great hymns of joy and belief. They knew that their loved one had moved on to a paradise with our Lord and was happy.

So, after we have sung our funeral or memorial services, our parade through the rest of our lives can sing songs of joy for the happiness that our dear ones now possess.

We can sing such songs as "Beams Of Heaven As I Go," "Forever With The Lord," "God Shall Wipe All The Tears Away," and "How Lovely Is Thy Dwelling Place."

Louis Armstrong would have joyously played "Oh, When The Saints Go Marching In."

Believers have spiritual lives that death cannot take away. Jesus promised us: "Because I live, you also will live" (John 14:19).

♪ A "Note" From The Choir Director ♪

Last year I had the privilege of teaching a music education course one night a week to the very fine young people at Trevecca College in Nashville.

One night I heard two boys running in the hall and actually falling *up* the stairs. One of them said as he ran, completely overcome with excitement, "We're doing the work of the Lord." I don't have the slightest idea as to what they were doing.

It brought tears to my eyes — tears of joy. To think that two young people were that excited about whatever their project was that one would want to say to the other as they ran, "We're doing the work of the Lord."

That reminds me that all of us need that kind of excitement in serving the church and our God. Whether that work be in singing in the choir or some other work, we need to fall *up* the stairs in excitement about it.

♪ A "Note" From The Choir Director ♪

We welcome our new pastor to our church. I couldn't help but think of something last Sunday when we met him in the choir room. That was the first time our new pastor heard the choir sing; and in trying to get that anthem ready for the service, you never sounded worse! Of course, when all got assembled, situated, and got into the service, you sang beautifully and with authority as you are able to do.

It reminded me of some recording sessions I have attended. Sometimes when a new artist comes to Nashville to record, the musicians have a little fun. Before the session begins, they sit there in the studio and play so badly in warming up that you can't believe it.

A while back, one of the great singers from the "Big Band Era" came to Music City to cut an album. On the first session with the artist, there is usually just a rhythm section. On later sessions, the "sweetening" is added (strings, horns, back-up singers, and so forth).

This singer walked into the studio for the first time. The musicians began to tune and warm up with the most horrible sound you ever heard. She didn't know whether to run, leave town, or what. But when the clock hit 10:00 and the session started, she was scared out of her mind by the most fantastic playing she had ever heard in her life.

I couldn't help but think of that last Sunday when you sounded unbelievably bad in rehearsal, but then went into the service where you ministered to the people with beauty, confidence, and authority.

Our worship service dealt with Pentecost and the Holy Spirit. Sunday we wanted to serve God and we wanted the Holy Spirit to help us. Life every day is like that. We can't do it alone. But with God's Spirit we can do things that may seem impossible.

♪ A "Note" From The Choir Director ♪

A week has passed since our special musical. Little did I know that you would go out there and sing the greatest, most nearly perfect performance of your lives. The letters and comments that have come to all of us prove that the Spirit of God expressed through your talents is what made it one of the most moving and inspiring musical services in the lives of the worshipers, as they have so expressed.

I must tell you of this little sidelight that I experienced. It seems that always I have been very fortunate in working with very fine people.

Lately I have been doing some work with a man named Joe. It is no secret to Joe that I am a Christian. Also, I learned that Joe was trained as a Free Will Baptist preacher and is presently serving a small church in another county to help the people get on their feet.

A week or ten days before our musical, I guess I mentioned the musical more than once to Joe. In fact, I don't know how much I may have mentioned it. Of course, I invited Joe and his wife to come to the service, but he has to preach at his church on Sunday nights.

Finally the morning rolled around following the service. When I saw Joe, the first thing he asked me was, "How did your service go?" He smiled at the excitement in my answer.

Then he said, "E. D., I thought of you last night about 6:00 knowing all of the planning you were having to get in order, so I spent a few prayer minutes for you and your church."

I was deeply touched to realize that a person I have known only a few weeks could be that concerned about me and my life and my church. I realize that is what Christianity is all about.

I want to ask all of you choir members as you finish reading this in the *Choir Notes*, to pray for Joe and his church. Thanks.

Number 7

♪ A "Note" From The Choir Director ♪

At the beginning of this month, I have been your choir director for one year.

I could look back and say thanks to you choir members for your loyalty. I could say thanks for your enthusiasm. I could say thanks for the good times and the good food at M.A.R.S. each month. I could say thanks for turning out on the rainy Wednesday nights (records will show that it has rained for over half of the Wednesday nights recently.) I could say thanks for all of this and more, and it would be true.

But mainly may I say that this past year my family and I have received a great blessing by being in your midst. We have made wonderful and lasting friendships. We have been inspired by you fellow Christians. And we have felt great love in God's House of Worship through the leadership of its pastors, and through the genuine spiritual sincerity with which you have raised your voices and expressed a text in your singing.

Our lives have been blessed.

♪ A "Note" From The Choir Director ♪

With the passing of Dr. Thor Johnson, not only the Nashville Symphony, but the entire world has lost a great music leader. Thor Johnson's father was a Moravian minister, and son Thor grew up with both the religious and the great musical uplifting of the Moravian culture.

I have played under many fine conductors in my life, but Thor Johnson impressed me the most. When I had to resign from playing with the symphony due to other conflicting endeavors, I told him with sincerity that he was a conductor who could verbalize his exact meanings to the orchestra which could make the players perform with feeling for his desired interpretation. He was a very educated man and had a genius for putting words together.

Thor Johnson when on the podium was very stern, authoritative, domineering, and a demander of great discipline. I respected him for this. Off the podium, he possessed the many Christian principles we recognize in kindness, gentleness, compassion, concern, and sincerity. He was a gentleman and he had class.

After I stopped playing with the orchestra, I did a great deal of work for Thor Johnson and the orchestra, such as copying scores they were to play, writing harmonizations, and writing parts with a change of key. I enjoyed this work and the relationship with him very much.

Thor Johnson called me from his hospital room a few days before Christmas. I was copying the parts to a Moravian Suite in fifteen movements which he was going to do on a recording session in January. He told me that he would need the score and parts by January 15. Incidentally, the fifteen different movements of the work were titled with such words as Anthem, Aria, Chorale, Arietta, and the like. But there was no title at the top of the score for the whole work.

So the last thing I said to him on the phone was, "By the way, what is the title of this suite?" Then the last words he ever spoke to me before his death were, "Psalm of Joy and Praise." I wished him a Merry Christmas and hung up.

Little did I know that soon after he would be gone. But I know for certainty that in that better world yet to come, away from the pain and affliction of the human body, he truly will be able to sing that "Psalm of Joy and Praise."

♪ A "Note" From The Choir Director ♪

This choir inspires me! I have been very pleased with our last few choir rehearsals. Then last Sunday's "God So Loved The World" by Stainer was a finished product of your rehearsing.

This thought occurred to me — as Christians it is our duty to be witnesses for God through our deeds and through our words. During each week I hope that each of us finds ways to witness with our deeds and our words.

But on Sunday morning in the church sanctuary, do you realize that we can stand on our feet and loudly proclaim such phrases as "I know that my Redeemer lives" and "Forbid it, Lord, that I should boast save in the death of Christ, my God" and "Love so amazing, so divine demands my soul, my life, my all."

This occurred to me last Sunday when the women had a soft section to sing and then the men came in with a stronger section proclaiming, "... that who so believeth in Him should not perish, but have everlasting life."

During the week we have to choose a different way to make our words and actions revealed to others as we witness. But on Sunday morning, do you realize what an opportunity we have?

See you Wednesday night.

♪ A "Note" From The Choir Director ♪

I have just finished a very interesting project. A while back, the John T. Benson Publishing Company in Nashville released some record albums called *Free Spirit*, which contain music for youth choirs in a contemporary idiom.

After the records were released, they wanted to publish choir books to go along with the records. It was my pleasure to make eleven of the piano transcriptions reduced from the orchestral scores to go in the choir books. The books now have been published.

It is hoped that the contemporary approach to the religious music will serve a real purpose with the youth. In fact, we hope all of the music in the church is varied enough to reach everyone.

I like these new books, *Free Spirit,* and I hope they minister unto and challenge the young, and inspire and reassure the old that the Spirit also enlightens and transforms a new generation, just as the publisher has stated on the record jacket.

♪ A "Note" From The Choir Director ♪

I feel like a treatise on "words"!

Last Wednesday night at rehearsal when we were working so hard on singing words expressively, I realized that I wanted to say even more about the importance of words in church music.

We have said it before, and all of us know the importance of words. But how many people sing a familiar hymn and don't pay any attention to the words? How many sing a song when they are engrossed in the beautiful melody and really don't know what the words mean?

Why shouldn't the choir minister unto the congregation through our words each worship service?

Words can say a lot to everyone. As in the music, there is a great variety of the way words can be spoken. Some words can be very sophisticated, some on a very high level of an intellectual attitude, some emotional, others spoken in a very simple way.

We hope that the variety of music that our choir does will speak words also in a variety of ways, whereby everyone may be touched by the presence of the Risen Christ.

Isn't it interesting to note that in the Bible, Jesus is referred to as the Word of God?

♪ A "Note" From The Choir Director ♪

Many people do not know very much about who their great grandparents or great-great-grandparents were, or even appear to be interested. I am not only interested, but I do know who many of my ancestors were.

For instance, my great-great-grandfather on my father's side was Reverend Miles Eddings Johnston. He was a devoted family man and a Methodist preacher.

I am thankful religion has played a great part in the lives of my family. My father's grandparents were James Thomas Ellis and Louisia Parlee Johnston Ellis. They lived in a small town called Shop Springs, Tennessee, which is not too far out in the country from our present home in Nashville.

Back in the days of my great-grandparents, people did not have a grocery store from which they could buy their staples and wares. Instead, a farmer would load up a wagon with fruit, vegetables, shoes, lamps, oil, household items, and other materials. He would hook his horse to a wagon and slowly move through the area selling the wares.

Lamps were the only source of light people had in those days. Everyone needed oil to keep them burning.

In the vicinity of Shop Springs, there were several small churches nestled between the rolling hills of our beautiful Tennessee. All of the churches, just like the homes in Shop Springs, depended on oil lamps.

Every Sunday morning when people went to their various churches, they were amazed to find that all of their lamps were full of oil and had been turned on. No one was able to find out who was filling those lamps with oil.

Finally, one day the mystery was solved. When my great-grandfather James Ellis died of a heart attack at age 65, all of the church people then realized that the oil lamps were left empty. He had never let anyone know that he had kept all of the church lamps full of oil.

♪ A "Note" From The Choir Director ♪

This may meet you with great sorrow, or with thunderous applause. I am writing to say that I have not written any "Note" from the choir director this issue. This is why:

I was driving along in my car thinking of what I was going to write for *Choir Notes* as the deadline was approaching. I was getting some ideas so that when I arrived at my office, I could quickly write it out.

While driving, I passed a car in trouble at the side of the road. A woman was standing by the car looking very distressed. I continued to drive on still thinking of what I would write for the *Choir Notes*. The thought did occur to me that the woman needed help. Of course, I was too busy to stop. After all, I was headed to my office to write some "good things" in my "Note from the Choir Director."

I went another block, and I was still nagged a little about helping that lady in trouble. Then it struck me! I thought, "What in the world am I doing? I am so busily running to write some of those 'good things' in the *Choir Notes* that I don't have time to stop and practice some of those 'good things' in my personal life."

Four blocks had now whizzed by. I found the nearest driveway so I could turn around. I did so, and headed back to the troubled person. When I got out of the car, I heard the lady take a deep breath and softly say, "Thank you, God."

To make the long story short, I took the time to help the lady in distress which left me no time to write "A 'Note' From The Choir Director" for this issue of *Choir Notes*.

♪ A "Note" From The Choir Director ♪

If I were a student and the English teacher required me to write an essay "On the Pipe Organ," I might express myself somewhat like this:

Last month we saw our pipe organ moved in piece by piece and were staggered by the amount of pipes, cables, and materials of all kinds.

The thing that struck a number of us was the precision, craft, yes — artistry which we could detect in each piece. Some of us picked up a small pipe and blew our own wind into it and heard how beautiful the quality of sound was even in the one pipe we were able to hold in our hands.

As I stood in the sanctuary one night when the organ was half installed, I felt the emotion of standing in the midst of a great piece of art. Just as we stand in awe before a masterful Michelangelo or Picasso, some day people will have that same emotion as they gaze upon the sculpture of this pipe organ, let alone hear the beauty of the sound.

Stereophonic sound is the combination of frequencies and timbre originating from two separate sources which give a living quality as it is received by the human ear. Quadrophonic sound originates from four sources.

Our pipe organ has sound originating from five separate locations, each enhancing the other. In the left chamber there are two large sections, one of which is "under expression," meaning that from the console the organist can open or shut the louver doors which change the quality. In the right chamber, all of the pipes are "under expression." And then there are the pipes on each side of the sanctuary which are exposed and we can see.

Every pipe is "voiced" individually after it gets in place. This is not left to chance. During the final week of installation, the voicer from the factory tunes and voices every pipe so that the quality of sound is enhanced by the specific architecture of our church structure where the pipe will stand. Therefore, there are no two pipe organs in the world exactly alike. This one belongs to our church.

Our service will be enhanced. Our worship will be more inspiring and meaningful. But let us always realize that the glory and dedication of service which this organ stands for belongs to God. We dedicate it to the Glory of God, and the service of all people, in the name and spirit of Jesus Christ, our Rightful Lord and Savior.

♪ A "Note" From The Choir Director ♪

Last Sunday night the Children's Choir sang a peppy song that surely put a smile on your face and made you tap your foot. I told the congregation to fasten their seat belts because this was going to be different. I told them that I felt Jesus would approve of it though.

We never have seen Jesus, but we know a lot about him from the Bible. We know that children ran to him and wanted to be with him. On at least one occasion when the children were being held back from him, Jesus said in effect, "No, let the children come to me." We know for a fact that children will not flock around a person who is gloomy, somber, and long-faced. So we must assume that Jesus must have been the happiest and jolliest fellow you ever saw for the children to want to come around him.

All of us need to come to Jesus as little children and have the faith of a little child. Sunday the choir will be singing an anthem that tells all about this to the congregation in song.

♪ A "Note" From The Choir Director ♪

We have a good church choir. And as long as you loyal members give your talents for the Lord to use in this way, we shall always have a good choir.

I recall a fine English teacher I had at one time who shocked me one day when she said, "E. D., stop reading good books." She said, "Why waste your time reading good books when there are so many great ones you can read."

Yes, we have a good choir. But why should we be content to have a good choir when we could have a great one?

What would this take? I am convinced that all it would take would be to have about fifteen more singers just like you. A large choir produces a quality which only numbers can produce. The joining together of many voices forms a physical timbre and combination of frequencies (that were divinely created, by the way) which effectuate a certain richness of quality that can be attained only by large numbers of combined voices. A small group cannot attain this quality of sound.

I salute you choir members not only for being a *good* choir, but for being on the edge of *greatness!*

♪ A "Note" From The Choir Director ♪

I want to report something about our trip to Miami Beach. I would like to say that we went to church that Sunday and could tell you about their choir, the sermon, and the service. But as a matter of fact, by the time we found out the location of a church, it was too far away and too late to get there. Being on Miami Beach without a car creates somewhat of a problem.

On the Sunday morning during church hour, our thoughts were with you. We walked down a street to see what was going on when everyone should be in church, and we came to a drug store.

We had no sooner gotten there when we heard some loud talking, screaming, and cursing. It seemed that a lady at the lunch counter was refusing to pay $2.05 for a sandwich. She said that she didn't want lettuce and tomato. She got up to leave, and the manager leaped over the counter and locked the front door to the store.

This lady slowly walked back to her sandwich on the counter still cursing, and sarcastically inquired of the manager, "What do you think this is, the Waldorf?" She reached over to sip a drink of water from her glass, and the manager knocked it out of her hand. Then real physical violence erupted with the manager saying, "Get out, you [expletives removed], and don't come back!"

We headed back to the hotel only to hear more altercations of varying nature and intensity on the street. Also, our path back encountered many drunks slumped over benches.

When hundreds of us are in church on Sunday mornings, there are thousands who are not even aware of the location of a church (as we found out by asking). So many lives are not touched by God's Spirit as is manifested in the number of people on the street showing hatred for their fellow beings rather than love. I heard *no* pleasant word from the mouth of anyone on that Sunday morning.

It concerns me. It should concern all Christians. What are we doing with our own lives to witness to others, to show the love of

God in our lives, and to bring peace, love, happiness, and salvation to their miserable lives?

I want us to give this some thought, and by the next issue of *Choir Notes*, let me list some of your suggestions. Think about it!

♪ A "Note" From The Choir Director ♪

The worship services in our church are very meaningful to me. I can truthfully say that *never* have I been at a worship service here when I didn't feel the presence of God.

I realize that this is true for many of us based on your comments, expressions, and the need for our "Tissue Brigade!" The music, the sermons, the prayers, and the responsive readings have made me feel the closeness of the Holy Spirit.

And do you realize, our worship begins at 10:40 A.M. in the choir room with our rehearsal followed always by a prayer from one of our pastors. I appreciate our pastors coming in and always having something very meaningful to say to us before we go into the sanctuary for the worship service.

I give thanks to the pastors and to you. Thanks to the pastors for their ministry and for realizing the importance of our music ministry in the worship services. Thanks to you for being of the loyal, dedicated quality which allows others to realize the importance of our ministry.

As the psalmist wrote: "I will sing to the Lord as long as I live; I will sing praise to my God while I have being" (Psalm 104:33).

♪ A "Note" From The Choir Director ♪

To say that we had a great vacation in Jamaica would be a masterpiece of an understatement. The people were friendly, their customs intriguing, the hotel comfortable, the pool wonderful, and the beautiful Caribbean Sea breathtaking.

Jeff and I were interested in the radio stations. We got to tour the Jamaica Broadcasting Company in Montego Bay. At night we could pick up the stations in Cuba, Mexico, South America, and a beautiful music station in the Cayman Islands. Also, there is a powerful Christian radio station in the Caribbean.

So many things are different in Jamaica from the United States. The people are different, their customs different, food is different, scenery different, language accent is different, money is different, and they even drive on the left side of the road. But when the Christian radio station comes on the air talking about Jesus, the story is the same!

♪ A "Note" From The Choir Director ♪

As the New Year approaches and the last few days of this year pass away, I look back over the year and say:

Thanks to the Sanctuary Choir members for their loyalty, dedication, service, and inspiration.

Thanks to our dedicated organist for his efficient and hard work.

Thanks to members of the Children's Choirs for praising God in song and making us realize that all of us must humble ourselves and come to God as little children in faith.

Thanks to members of the Youth Choir for bringing their energy and enthusiasm and personal testimony to others.

Thanks to the teachers, sponsors, and leaders of all the choirs for their fine leadership and their love for their children.

Thanks to the many handbell ringers and other instrumentalists who have been added blessings to our worship services.

Thanks to my wife Sonia, my son Jeff, my daughter Lee Anne, and their puppet Crescendo Coyote for making the children's choirs a happy and spiritual experience for our little ones.

Thanks to our pastor and shepherd for his sincere and total concern for his flock.

Thanks to the church staff for its dedication and efficient service.

Thanks to our church for its leadership in our city.

Thanks to God for the constant outpouring of love, blessings, and especially the gift of his Son.

Happy New Year!